Peter Pullman

The Age of

Suspicion

The Age of Suspicion

Essays on the Novel

by

Nathalie Sarraute

Translated by Maria Jolas

George Braziller   *New York, 1963*

Contents

From

Dostoievski

to

Kafka

The novel, we constantly hear it said today, falls into two quite distinct categories: the psychological novel and the novel "in situation." On the one hand, Dostoievski and, on the other, Kafka. Indeed, if we are to believe Roger Grenier,[1] even the news-item—and this illustrates Oscar Wilde's famous paradox—divides quite naturally into these two genres. However, in life as well as in literature, Dostoievski characters (or so it appears) are becoming less fre-

[1] Roger Grenier, "Utilité du fait divers" ("Utility of the news-item"), *Temps Modernes,* No. 17, p. 95.

quent. "The genius of our epoch," M. Grenier notes, "inclines in favor of Kafka . . . and even in Soviet Russia, Dostoievski figures are no longer to be seen in the court rooms." Today, he declares, we are faced with *"homo absurdus, the lifeless inhabitant of a century whose prophet is Kafka."*

This dearth of what is called with a certain irony "the psychological" (held between quotes as though between tongs), and which, it seems, is due to the lot of modern man who, being overwhelmed by our mechanical civilization, is reduced, according to Claude-Edmonde Magny, "to the triple determinism of hunger, sexuality and social status: Freud, Marx and Pavlov," seems, nevertheless, to have inaugurated for both writer and reader an era of security and hope.

The time was well past when Proust had boldly believed that "by urging his impression on as far as his powers of penetration would allow" (he could) "try to reach the ultimate deep where lie truth, the real universe, our most authentic impression." Having learned the lesson of successive disappointments, everybody knew now that there was no ultimate deep. "Our

12

authentic impression" had been found to have any number of depths; and they extended one beneath the other, *ad infinitum.*

The deep uncovered by Proust's analyses had already proved to be nothing but a surface. A surface too, the one that the interior monologue, basis of so many legitimate hopes, had succeeded in identifying. And the immense progress achieved by psychoanalysis, which stopped at nothing, passing through several depths at one time, had shown the inefficacy of classic introspection, and inspired doubts as to the ultimate value of all methods of research.

Homo absurdus, therefore, was Noah's dove, the messenger of deliverance.

Now, at last, it was permissible to leave behind without remorse all sterile endeavor, all wearisome floundering, all nerve-racking splitting of hairs; modern man, having become a soulless body tossed about by hostile forces, was nothing, when all was said and done, but what he appeared to be on the surface. The inexpressive torpor, the immobility that a quick glance could observe in his face when he let himself go, hid no interior reactions. The "tumult like unto silence" that adherents of "the psychological" had thought they saw in his soul was nothing, after all, but silence.

His consciousness was composed of nothing but a superficial network of "conventional opinions taken over just as they were from the group to which he belonged," and these very commonplaces hid "a profound nothingness," an almost total "absence from self." The so-called "heart of hearts," the "ineffable intimacy with oneself," had been nothing but a delusion and a snare. "The psychological," which had been the source of such great disappointment and sorrow, did not exist.

This soothing conclusion brought with it the delightful sense of restored vigor and optimism that usually accompanies liquidations and renunciations.

Now it was possible to gather one's forces and, forgetting past misadventures, start over again, "on new bases." On every side, more accessible, pleasanter prospects seemed to be opening up. The very promising art of the cinema would allow the novel which, as a result of so many fruitless efforts, had reassumed a touching, juvenile modesty, to benefit by its entirely new techniques. By virtue of a beneficent contagion, the wholesome simplicity of the new American novel, with its somewhat unpolished vigor, would restore a certain vitality and sap to our own, which had become weakened by over-indulgence in analysis, and was threatened with senile desiccation. The literary object would be able to recapture the full outlines, the hard, smooth, finished aspect of fine classical works. The "poetic" and purely descriptive elements in which the novelist too often saw merely vain ornamentation, and which he only parsimoniously allowed to pass after minute filtering, would lose its humiliating rôle of auxiliary, exclusively subject to the demands of psychology, and blossom out any-and-everywhere, unrestrained. By the same token, style, to the immense satisfaction of those "persons of taste" who inspired such fearful apprehensions in Proust, would recover the pure lines and sober elegance that are so little compatible with the contortions and stampings, the finespun subtleties, or the mired ponderousness of "the psychological."

And, quite close to us, Kafka, whose message combined so felicitously with that of the Americans, showed what still-unexplored regions could open up for the writer, once he was rid of the unfortunate nearsightedness that had forced him to examine each object at close range, and kept him from seeing further than the end of his own nose.

Lastly, those who, despite all these assurances and promises, still had certain scruples, and continued to lend an anxious ear, to be convinced that behind that dead silence there subsisted no echo of the former tumult, could feel fully reassured.

Contrary to the formless, soft matter that yields and disintegrates under the scalpel of analysis, this fragment of the universe within whose boundaries the new novel prudently remained confined, formed a hard, compact whole that was absolutely indivisible. Its very hardness and opacity preserved its interior complexity and density and conferred upon it a force of penetration that allowed it to attain not to the superficial, arid regions of the reader's intellect, but to those infinitely fertile, "listless and defenseless regions of the sentient soul." It provoked a mysterious, salutary shock, a sort of emotional commotion that made it possible to apprehend all at once, and as in a flash, an entire object with all its nuances, its possible complexities, and even—if, by chance, these existed —its unfathomable depths. There was therefore nothing to lose and, apparently, everything to be gained.

When Albert Camus' *The Stranger* appeared, it was permissible to believe with good reason that it would fulfill all hopes. Like all works of real value it came at the appointed time; it responded to our expectations; it crystallized all our suspended stray impulses. From now on, we need envy no one. We too had our *homo absurdus*. And he enjoyed the undeniable advantage over even Dos Passos' and Steinbeck's heroes of being depicted not at a distance and from the outside, as they were, but from within, through the classical process of introspection, so dear to adherents of "the psychological": we could ascertain his inner nothingness at close range and, as it were, from a front box. In fact, as Maurice Blanchot wrote,[1] "This Stranger's relation to himself is as though someone else were observing and speaking of him . . . He is entirely on the outside, and all the more himself in that he seems to think less, feel less, be less intimate with

[1] Maurice Blanchot, *Faux Pas*, pp. 257 and 259.

his self. The very image of human reality when it is stripped of all psychological conventions, when we try to grasp it by a description made solely from the outside, deprived of all false, subjective explanations . . ." And Claude Edmonde Magny wrote[1]: "Camus wants to let us see the inner nothingness of his hero and, through it, our own nothingness . . . Meursault is man stripped of all the ready-made garments with which society clothes the normal void of his being: his conscience . . . The sentiments and psychological reactions he tries to find in himself (sadness as his mother lies dying, love for Maria, remorse at the murder of the Arab) he does not find: indeed, all he finds is a view that is absolutely similar to the view that others may have of his behavior."

And the fact is that during this scene of his mother's funeral, although he does occasionally discover within himself a few of the sentiments that classical analysis, albeit with a certain timorous fluster, succeeded in uncovering; a few of the fugitive thoughts, "shadowy and shy," that it detected (among so many others) "gliding by

[1] Cl. Edmonde Magny, "Roman américain et Cinéma," *Poésie 45,* No. 24, p. 69.

with the furtive speed of fish"—such as the pleasure he derives from a lovely morning in the country, the disappointment he feels at the thought of the outing this funeral has made him miss, or the memory of what he usually does at this time of morning—on the contrary, everything that in any way concerns his mother, and not only ordinary sorrow (without surprising us too much, he might have experienced a sense of deliverance and satisfaction, like one of Virginia Woolf's heroines), but all sentiment or thought whatsoever, appears to have been completely abolished, as though by a magic wand. In this well-scrubbed, well-adorned conscience, there is not the slightest scrap of memory that ties back to childhood impressions, not the palest shadow of those ready-made sentiments that the very persons who think they are best protected against conventional emotions and literary reminiscences, feel slip through them.

This state of anesthesia appears to be so profound that we are reminded of the patients described by Dr. Janet, who suffer from what he has called "feelings of emptiness," and who keep saying: "All my feelings have disappeared . . . My head is empty . . . My heart is empty . . . people and things are a matter of equal indifference to me . . . I can go through all the motions, but, in doing so, I feel neither joy nor sorrow . . . Nothing tempts me, nothing disgusts me . . . I am a living statue; whatever happens to me, it is impossible for me to have a sensation or a sentiment about anything . . ."

Despite these similarities of language, however, there is nothing in common between Albert Camus' character and Dr. Janet's patients. Meursault who, in certain things, appears to be so insensitive, so simple-minded and as though in a daze, in certain others, gives evidence of refinement of taste and exquisite delicacy. The very style in which he expresses himself makes him, rather than the rival of Steinbeck's bellowing hero, the heir to the *Princess of Cleve* and *Adolph*. As the Abbé Brémond would say, he is "all strewn with winter roses." This Stranger has the vigorous acuity of line, the rich palette of a great painter: "Without a smile she inclined her long, bony face . . ." "I was a bit lost between the blue and white sky and the monotony of these colors, the sticky black of the fresh tar, the dull black of people's clothes, the enamel black of the car" . . . He notes with the tenderness of a

20

poet the delicate play of light and shadow and the varying tints of the sky. He recalls the "brimming sun that made the landscape quiver," "an odor of night and flowers." He hears a "moan that became slowly audible like a flower born of silence." Unerring taste guides the choice of his epithets. He speaks of "a drowsy headland," "a *dark* breath."

But there are things that are still more disturbing. If we are to judge by the details that hold his attention—such as the episode of the maniac or, above all, the one about old Salamano, who hates and martyrizes his dog and, at the same time, loves it with deep, moving tenderness—he is not averse to skirting about the edges of the abyss, with prudence, of course, and circumspection. Despite the "ingenuousness" and "unconsciousness" with which he discloses, to quote Maurice Blanchot, that "man's real, constant mood is: I do not think, I have nothing to think about," he is much more aware than we imagine. As witness, such a remark as this, that he lets drop: "All healthy human beings (have) more or less wished for the death of those they loved," which shows that, on occasion, and doubtless oftener than most, he has made rather deep incursions into forbidden, dangerous zones.

The feeling of malaise that we are unable to shake off all through the book probably comes from these very apparent contradictions, and only at the end when, incapable of containing himself any longer, Camus' hero feels that "something . . . has burst inside (him)" and "he pours out . . . all the depths of (his) heart," do we feel, with him, a sense of release: ". . . I appeared to have empty hands. But I was sure of myself, sure of everything . . . sure of my life and of this death that was going to come . . . I had been right, I was still right, I was always right . . . What did the death of others mean to me, or a mother's love; what was the meaning of the lives we choose, the fates we elect, since one single fate had elected me and, with me, billions of privileged people . . . Everybody was privileged . . . There were nothing but privileged people . . . One day the others too would be condemned."

Now we have it. Finally! What we had timidly surmised is suddenly confirmed. This young employee, who is so simple and rough-hewn, in whom we were asked to recognize the new, long-awaited man, was, in reality, diametrically opposed to him. His attitude which, at times, may possibly have recalled the stubborn negativism of a sulky child, was one of determined, haughty prejudice, a desperate, lucid refusal, an example and perhaps, too, a lesson. The willful frenzy, characteristic of genuine intellectuals, with which he cultivates pure sensation, his very conscious egoism, fruit of some tragic experience that, thanks to this exceptional sensitivity of his, has left him with a fine, constant sense of nothingness (had he not given us to understand that formerly, "when (he was) a student, (he had had) great ambitions . . ." but that "after (he had) been obliged to leave school, (he had) very soon understood that none of that was really important") relate *The Stranger* to Gide's *The Immoralist.*

Thus, by way of analysis, and of the psychological explanations that, up till the last moment, Camus took such pains to avoid, the contradictions and improbabilities of his book are explained, and the emotion to which we yield at last, unreservedly, is justified.

Camus' situation recalls somewhat that of King Lear, taken in charge by the least favored of his daughters. For, in the end, it is to the "psychological," which he had tried so carefully to root out, but which came up again everywhere like weeds, that he owes his salvation.

But however relieved we may feel, when we have closed the book, we cannot help harboring a certain resentment against the author: we begrudge him the fact of having led us too long astray. His behavior toward his character reminds us a bit too much of certain mothers who persist in dressing their buxom and already adult daughters in skirts that are too short. In this unequal struggle, the "psychological," like nature, came out on top.

But perhaps, on the contrary, Camus was trying to demonstrate a wager on the impossibility, in our climes, of doing without psychology. If this was his purpose, he more than succeeded.

But, people will say, what about Kafka? Who would maintain that his *homo absurdus* was nothing but a mirage? There is no willfulness in his attitude, no concern for didactics, no prejudice. He doesn't need to go in for impossible labors of weeding: on the bare lands to which he leads us, no blade of grass can grow.

Yet nothing is more arbitrary than to compare him, as is often done today, with the writer who was, if not his teacher, at least his precursor, as he was for nearly all the European writers in our time, whether they realize it or not.

Across the immense territories opened up by Dostoievski, Kafka drew a path, a single, long, narrow path; he advanced in a single direction, and followed it to the end. To be assured of this, we must rise above our reluctance, turn backward a moment and plunge into the very thick of the tumult. In the presence of a numerous gathering, the elder Karamazov enters the highly respected Father Zossima's cell and introduces himself: "You see before you a buffoon, a real buffoon! That's how I present myself . . . an old habit, alas!" and he starts to writhe, makes faces, a sort of St. Vitus dance dislocates all his movements, he assumes ludicrous poses, describes with savage, bitter lucidity how he has put himself in humiliating situations, using, in speaking, those humble and, at the same time, aggressive diminutives, those little saccharine, corrosive words that so many of Dostoievski's characters affect; he lies brazenly, and when caught in the act, falls on his feet again . . . he can never be taken off his guard, he knows himself: "I knew it, imagine, and do you know, I even sensed it as

soon as I started talking, and I also even sensed
(because he has strange premonitions) that you
would be the first to point it out to me," he is
lowering himself even more, as though he knew
that, in this way, he lowers and abases the others
too, he sneers, begins to confess his sins: "it was
just now, at this very instant, while I was talking,
that I invented everything . . . to make it sound
more pithy," because, like an ill person who is
constantly on the alert for symptoms of his ill-
ness, his eyes turned on himself, he is examining,
watching himself: it is to coax them, to win them
over, to disarm them, that he carries on this way,
"it's to be more agreeable that I make faces, in
fact sometimes I myself don't know why." As he
continues to go round and round, he makes us
think of certain clowns who, without stopping
their pirouetting, take off their clothes, one gar-
ment after another: "in fact, I don't know, there
may also be an evil spirit in me," and he starts
crawling again: "oh, a little one, to be sure, if
he were bigger he would have chosen another
home," then immediately pulls himself up and
snarls, "not yours, you too are a sorry home."
The Staretz tries to lay a calming hand on him
. . . "Let me urge you not to feel uncomfortable

26

or ill at ease, make yourself quite at home . . .
And above all (for he too is examining closely,
without a shadow of indignation or loathing,
this turgid matter that is boiling up and over-
flowing), and above all, don't be so ashamed of
yourself, because it only comes from that."—
"Quite at home, really? that is to say, perfectly
natural? Oh, that's too much, far too much, I myself would not go that far." He makes an obscene
schoolboy joke and immediately grows serious
again: the Staretz has understood him, he con-
torts himself like that to conform to the idea they
have of him, to outbid them, "because it seems
to me, when I approach people . . . that everybody takes me for a buffoon. So I say to myself:
why not act the buffoon, then . . . because all of
you, to the very last one, you are lower than I
am, and that's why I am a buffoon . . . it is out
of shame, Father, out of shame . . ." A moment
later, he falls on his knees, and "it is hard, even
then, to know whether he is joking or deeply
moved: 'Master, what must I do to gain eternal
life?' The Staretz comes a little nearer: 'Above
all, do not lie to yourself . . . he who lies to himself . . . is the first to be offended . . . he knows
that no one has offended him . . . and yet he is

27

offended to the point of feeling satisfaction, immense pleasure' . . ." Being an experienced con-
noisseur, Karamazov weighs this statement.
"Exactly, exactly, I have felt offended all my life,
to the point of enjoyment, for its aesthetic value,
because it is not only agreeable, but sometimes it
is exquisite to be offended . . . you forget that,
Father: it is exquisite!" . . . He leaps up, makes
another pirouette and casts off another harle-
quin's costume: "You think that I always lie
like this and act the buffoon? I want you to know
that it was on purpose, to test you, that I in-
dulged in this play-acting. I was trying you out
. . . is there room for my humility beside your
pride? . . ."

Emerging from this whirlwind, we are obliged
to admire the credit that adherents of the
method that consists in being content to skirt
prudently around the object from the outside,
must grant the reader (thus conceding to him
what, by a curious contradiction, they refuse
their characters) when they imagine that, even
after reading a long novel, he can possibly perceive, through some sort of magic intuition, so
much as a part of what the six pages of which we
have just given a very rough summary, have
shown him.

All of these strange contortions—and we should reproach ourselves for pointing this out, if there were not still those today who, like Paul Léautaud, allow themselves to speak seriously of "that lunatic Dostoievski"—all of these disordered leapings and grimacings, are the absolutely precise, outward manifestation, reproduced without indulgence or desire to please, the way the magnetic needle of a galvanometer gives amplified tracings of the minutest variations of a current, of those subtle, barely perceptible, fleeting, contradictory, evanescent movements, faint tremblings, ghosts of timid appeals and recoilings, pale shadows that flit by, whose unceasing play constitutes the invisible woof of all human relationships and the very substance of our lives.

Of course the methods that Dostoievski used to reproduce these subjacent movements were primitive ones. If he had lived in our time, the more delicate instruments of investigation at the disposal of modern techniques would no doubt have permitted him to seize these movements at their source, thus avoiding all these incredible gesticulations. But by using our techniques, he might also have lost more than he gained. They would have inclined him toward greater realism and finer minutiae, but he would have lost his originality and ingenuous boldness of line; he would have sacrificed something of his poetic force of evocation, as well as of his tragic power.

And it should be said immediately that what is revealed by these starts and sudden changes, these pirouettings, premonitions and confessions, has absolutely no relation to the disappointing, abstract exposure of motives to which our methods of analysis are accused of leading today. These subjacent movements, this incessant swirl, similar to the movement of atoms, that all of these grimaces bring to light, are themselves nothing else but action, and they only differ by their delicacy, their complexity and their "underground" nature—to use one of Dostoievski's favorite words—from the larger, close-up actions we are shown in a Dos Passos novel, or in a film.

We find these same movements again in different degrees of intensity, and with infinite variations, in all of Dostoievski's characters: in the hero of *Notes from Underground,* in Hippolite or Lebedieff, in Grouchenka or Rogojine, and above all, only more precise, more complicated, more delicate and broader than elsewhere, in the

Eternal Husband. Here, it will be recalled, we have the same furtive starts, the same skillful thrusts, the same feints, the same mock quarrels, the same attempts at rapprochement, the same extraordinary presentiments, the same provocations, the same subtle, mysterious game in which hatred mingles with tenderness, revolt and fury with childlike docility, abjectness with the most authentic pride, cunning with ingenuousness, extreme delicacy with extreme rudeness, familiarity with deference; Pavlovitch teases, provokes, attacks, crawls, lies in wait, flees when sought, remains when driven out, tries to touch people's hearts, then immediately bites, weeps and shows his love, dedicates himself, sacrifices himself, and, a few seconds later, leans over, razor in hand, to kill; he speaks in the same saccharine, slightly mocking and obsequious manner, a speech that is larded with crawling, aggressive diminutives, with words servilely prolonged by those hissing suffixes that, in the Russian language of the time, denoted a sort of acrid, sweetish deference; then, occasionally drawing himself up to all his manly height, he dominates, bestows, generously pardons, overwhelms.

These attitudes are repeated so often in countless different situations, throughout Dostoievski's works, that we might almost reproach him with a certain monotony. In fact, at times we have the impression of being in the presence of a veritable obsession.

"All of these characters," wrote Gide,[1] "are cut from the same cloth. Pride and humility remain the secret motives of everything they do, although differences of dosage give varied reactions." But it appears that humility and **pride** are also mere modalities, mere shadings, and that underneath them there is another, still more secret motive, a movement of which pride and humility are but repercussions. It is doubtless to this initial movement, which lends impulse to all the others, to this spot at which all the trunk lines that traverse this tumultuous mass converge, that Dostoievski alluded when he spoke of his "source," "my eternal source," from which he derived, as he said, "the material for each one of my works, even though their form be different." This meeting place, this "source," is rather hard to define. We might perhaps convey an idea of it by saying that, when all is said and done,

[1] André Gide, *Dostoievski*, p. 145.

it is nothing but what Katherine Mansfield called, with some fear and, perhaps, slight distaste: "this terrible desire to establish contact."

It is this continual, almost maniacal need for contact, for an impossible, soothing embrace, that attracts all of these characters like dizziness and incites them on all occasions to try, by any means whatsoever, to clear a path to the "other," to penetrate him as deeply as possible and make him lose his disturbing, unbearable opaqueness; in their turn, it impels them to confide in him and show him their own innermost recesses. Their momentary dissimulations, their furtive leaps, their secretiveness, their contradictions, the inconsistencies of their conduct, which, at times, they appear to multiply for the mere pleasure of it, and dangle before the eyes of the other, are, in their case, nothing but coy, flirtatious attempts to arouse his curiosity and oblige him to draw nearer. Nor is their humility anything but a timid, round-about appeal, a way of showing that they are quite near, accessible, disarmed, open, acquiescent, in complete surrender, completely abandoned to the understanding, the generosity, of the other: all the barriers erected by dignity, by vanity, have been torn down, anyone can approach them, no one need fear to come in, entrance is free. And their sudden starts of pride are merely painful attempts, in the face of an intolerable refusal, a rejection of their appeal, when the path their humility had tried to follow is closed, to quickly back away and, by choosing other means of access, through hatred, contempt, inflicted suffering, or through some brilliant feat, some bold, generous gesture that astounds and dumbfounds people, succeed in re-establishing contact, in re-assuming possession of the other.

This incapacity to take their place to one side, at a distance, to stand "on their dignity," in a state of opposition, or of just plain indifference, is the source of their strange malleability, of that curious docility with which, constantly, as though they were trying to wheedle and win people over, they take as their model the image of themselves that others reflect back to them. This is also the source of that strange impulse that constantly impels those who feel debased to debase themselves even further and force others to wallow in the same debasement. If, as André Gide observes,[1] "they do not know how, they are

[1] *Id.*, p. 185.

incapable of being jealous" and if "all they know about jealousy is suffering," it is because the rivalry implied by jealousy produces the unbearable antagonism, the break, that they seek to avoid at all cost; in consequence, this rivalry, in their case, is continually being destroyed, submerged under a curious kind of tenderness, or under that very special sentiment that can hardly be called hatred, which, with them, is simply a way of approaching one's rival, of grasping, of clasping, him to oneself by means of the object of their love.

This refusal to consider their claim, this "wise don't understand" that Rilke speaks of and concerning which he adds that it means "accepting to be alone, (whereas) struggle and contempt are ways of participating," in their case, are rarely met with. Contact is inevitably established, the appeal is always heard. Nor does the reply ever fail to come, whether it be in the form of an impulse toward tenderness and forgiveness, or toward struggle and contempt.

For although for certain privileged characters, such as Alyosha, Father Zossima or the Idiot, the roads that lead to their neighbor are the broad straight roads of love, others, less fortunate, find only muddy, winding roads before them; and some can only walk backward, stumbling over countless obstacles. All, however, have the same goal.

They all respond, they all understand. Each one knows that he is nothing but a fortuitous, more or less felicitous assemblage of elements derived from the same common source, that all the others harbor within themselves his own possibilities, his own stray impulses; this explains why each one of them judges the actions of others as he would his own, at close range, and from within, with all their countless shadings and contradictions which prevent classification and indiscriminate labeling; why no one can ever have the panoramic view of the conduct of others that, alone, makes rancor and blame permissible; it explains the disturbed curiosity with which each one continually scrutinizes the souls of others; the astonishing premonitions, presentiments, the clear-sightedness, the supernatural gift of penetration, which are not the sole privilege of those who are enlightened by Christian love, but of all these dubious characters, these parasites with their saccharine, bitter talk, these larvae who continue to dig and stir in the very dregs of the soul and sniff with delight its nauseous slime.

Crime itself, assassination, which is a sort of ultimate end of all these movements, the bottom of the abyss toward which they all continue to lean, fearful and attracted, is merely, in their case, the supreme embrace, and the only definitive break. But even this supreme break may yet be repaired thanks to public confession, by means of which the criminal deposits his crime in the common patrimony.

In fact, in all of Dostoievski's works, with perhaps one single exception, no definitive break, no irreparable separation, ever occurs.

If, here and there, one of the two partners permits himself too great a deviation in conduct, or is so bold as to remain aloof and look down upon the other, the way Veltchaninov does in *The Eternal Husband* when, "the game" having been up for a long time, he becomes again the satisfied man of the world he had been formerly, before the game started, a brief call to order suffices (a hand that refuses to be stretched out, four words: "and what about Lisa?") for the polite varnish to crack and fall away, and contact to be re-established.

In only one of his stories—and it is also the only one that is really despairing—the *Notes from Underground,* which is situated, as it were, on the very confines, in the extreme forefront of his entire oeuvre, because of the pitiless refusal the man underground meets with on the part of his comrades, narrow-minded, dull little civil servants, and the young officer, Zverkov, the root of whose name is a word that means "animal" or "beast," with the stupid head of a ram and elegant, clever, self-assured manners, full of a remote sort of politeness, who "examines him in silence as though he were some curious insect," while he carries on before them, hurling in vain his shameful, ludicrous appeals at them—here, it will be recalled, the break does occur.

This continual need to establish contact— which is one of the primal characteristics of the Russian people, in whom Dostoievski's work is so firmly rooted—has contributed to making of Russian soil the chosen soil, the veritable black loam of "the psychological."

Indeed, nothing could be better calculated than are these impassioned questions and answers, these attractions, these feigned withdrawals, these pursuits and flights, these flirtings and rubbings, these clashes, caresses, bites and embraces, to excite, disturb, bring up to the surface and allow to spread, the immense, quivering mass, whose incessant ebb and flow, whose scarcely perceptible vibration, are the very pulse of life.

Under the pressure of this tumult, the envelope that contains it wears thin and tears. There occurs a sort of displacement from outside inward, from the center of gravity of the character, a displacement which the modern novel has never ceased to stress.

Many have noted the impression of unreality —as though we saw them transparently—that Dostoievski's characters make upon us, despite the minute descriptions that he felt obliged to give in order to satisfy the demands of his epoch.

This comes from the fact that his characters tended already to be what, more and more, characters in fiction were to become, that is, not so much "types" of flesh-and-blood human beings, like those we see around us, to enumerate whom seemed to be the novelist's essential goal, as simple props, carriers of occasionally still unexplored states of consciousness, which we discover within ourselves.

It may be that Proust's snobbishness, which recurs in an almost maniacally besetting manner in all of his characters, is nothing but a variety of this same need of fusion, only grown and cultivated in a very different soil, in the formal, refined society of the Faubourg St. Germain, at the beginning of this century. In any case, Proust's works show us already that these complex, subtle states (we should say, these movements) the slightest shadings of which, in the anxiety of his quest, he has succeeded in capturing in all his characters, remain what is most precious and soundest in his work; while the envelopes, which were perhaps a bit too thick—Swann, Odette, Oriane de Guermantes, or the Verdurins—are already on the way to the vast waxworks to which, sooner or later, all literary "types" are relegated.

But, to return to Dostoievski, these movements upon which all his attention, that of all his characters and also of the reader, are concentrated; which derive from a common source, and despite the envelopes separating them from one another, like little drops of mercury, continually tend to conglomerate and mingle with the common mass; these roving states which, from one character to another, traverse the entire oeuvre, are to be found in everybody, refracted in each one of us according to a different index, and each time they present us one of their as yet unknown, innumerable facets, thus allowing us to sense something that might foreshadow a sort of new unanimism.

The tie between this work, which is still a living source of research and new techniques, still rich in promise, and the work of Kafka, to which people tend to contrast it today, appears evident, and if literature were to be regarded as a continuous relay race, it would no doubt have been from Dostoievski's hands, more certainly than from those of any other, that Kafka would have seized the token.

It will be recalled that his K., whose very name is reduced to a mere initial, is but a slender prop. And the sentiment or cluster of sentiments gathered and held together by this frail envelope are nothing if not this same passionate, anxious desire to establish contact that runs like a guiding thread through Dostoievski's entire work. But whereas the quest on which Dostoievski's characters are bent leads them to seek a sort of interpenetration, a total and ever possible fusion of souls, in the most fraternal of worlds, the entire effort of Kafka's heroes is aimed at a goal that is at once less ambitious and less attainable. All they want is to become, "in the eyes of these people who regard them with such distrust . . . not their friend, perhaps, but in any case, their fellow citizen" . . . , to be able to appear and justify themselves before unknown, unapproachable accusers, or to seek to safeguard, despite all obstacles, some paltry semblance of a relationship with those closest to them.

This humble pursuit, by virtue of its desperate obstinacy, of the depths of human suffering, the distress and complete abandonment that it brings to light, extends well beyond the domain of psychology and lends itself to all kinds of metaphysical interpretations.

However, readers who would like to assure themselves that Kafka's heroes have no connection with those characters in fiction whose authors, out of a need to simplify, through prejudice or from didactical motives, have emptied them of "all subjective thought and life," and present them as "the very image of human reality when it is divested of all psychological conventions," need only re-read the minute, subtle analyses that Kafka's characters indulge in with impassioned lucidity, as soon as the slightest contact is established between them. As, for instance, the skillful dissections of K.'s conduct and sentiments toward Freida, performed with the keenest of blades, first by the landlady, then by Freida, then by K. himself, and which reveal the complicated interplay of delicate wheelworks, a flash of multiple and often contradictory intentions, impulses, calculations, impressions and presentiments.

But these moments of sincerity, these states of grace, are as rare as the contacts that may give rise to them (love between Frieda and K.—if their strange relationship may be so called—or hatred for K. on the part of the landlady).

If we were to try to locate the exact spot in Dostoievski's writings at which Kafka "seized the token," it would no doubt be found in the *Notes from Underground* which, as we have seen, constitutes a sort of ultimate limit, the furthermost point of this oeuvre.

The hero of these *Notes* knows that, for the officer who "takes him by the shoulders and without any explanation, without a word, moves him to one side and passes on, as though he did not exist," he is now nothing but a mere object, or, in the eyes of Zverkov, with his "ram's head," a "curious insect"; as he tries to mingle with the crowd and "slips between the passers-by in the most odious way," he feels "like an insect"; he becomes very clearly aware that, in their midst, he is nothing but a "fly," "a nasty fly." This furthermost point at which he finds himself for a very brief moment—for he will quickly be revenged, he will discover within easy reach human beings with whom the closest fusion will always be possible (such as Lisa, whom he will immediately cause to suffer, and by whom he will succeed in making himself both intensely loved and hated)—this furthermost point to which he is driven for an instant only, will be the same world without exit, enlarged to the dimensions of an endless nightmare, in which Kafka's characters will flounder.

We all know this world, in which a sinister game of blindman's buff is in constant progress, in which people always advance in the wrong direction, in which outstretched hands "claw the void," in which everything we touch eludes us, in which the person we clutch for a moment and feel with uneasy hands, suddenly becomes transferred or escapes, in which appeals are always misleading, in which questions are left unanswered, in which "the others" are those who throw you out "without a word, but with the greatest possible force," because "hospitality is not practiced" among them, they "do not need guests," those who look without flinching, or absent-mindedly forget to see the hand you "hold outstretched, thinking all the while that they are going to take it," those who, when you ask them "if you can't come to see them (because) you feel a bit lonely," content themselves with giving their address "for your information, rather than as an invitation," those who, if you come to sit beside them, say: "I shall be leaving," those who, in your presence, speak of you as though you were an object, and observe your movements, "to which even horses react, as though they were watching the comings and goings of a cat," those who, one fine day, as Klamm did with the landlady—and without years and years, an entire life of uneasy reflection ever making it possible for you to understand "how it happened"—break off all connection with you, "never call you again and never will call you"; in which "the others" are half-human creatures with identical faces, whose childish, incomprehensible gestures, underneath their apparent naïveté and disorder, conceal a malicious sort of cleverness that is at once cunning and obtuse; these are the enigmatically smiling men who observe you from a distance with sly, childish curiosity, who look at you "without speaking to one another, each man for himself, with no other tie than the target they are looking at," who move away docilely when they are driven off, then immediately return to their places with the mechanical, passive obstinacy of tumbler dolls; a world in which, above everything, "the others," those toward whom we strain with all our might, are "remote and invisible" "gentlemen," occupying administrative functions that are minutely and strictly stratified in hierarchic order, simple wheels within wheels *ad infinitum,* up to the central wheel of a mysterious organization which, for unknown reasons, is the only one that can grant or refuse you the right to exist; civil servants the meanest of whom wields over you, who are nothing "but a pitiful subject, a shade . . . wretchedly buried in the most distant of distances," infinite power.

46

These "gentlemen" whom it is impossible to know even by sight, whom you can watch for vainly your entire life long, who "will never speak to you and never allow you to appear before them, whatever pains you may take and however insistently you may importune them," with whom you cannot hope to establish any sort of relationship other than "to be mentioned in an official report" which they will probably never read, but which, at least, "will be filed in their records," themselves have only a distant knowledge of you, which is both general and precise, like the information to be found in the card-index of a penitentiary director's office.

Here, where distances as immense as interplanetary space separate human beings from one another, where you constantly have "the impression that all connection with you has been broken off," all landmarks disappear, your sense of orientation becomes dulled, little by little your movements become disordered, your sentiments disintegrate (what remains of love is nothing but a savage tussle in which the lovers, under the indifferent gaze of the spectators, "make desperate assault on each other, disappointed, powerless to help," or else, a few

47

abrupt, mechanical gestures, parodies of caresses, directed toward an anonymous partner, like those that Leni lavishes upon K., because he is under accusation and, to her, all defendants are admirable), words lose their usual meaning and efficacy, attempts at justification only serve to prove your guilt, approval is a trap "to lead the innocent into temptation"; "everything is falsely interpreted," even to your own questions, you no longer understand your own conduct, "you do not know whether you resisted or yielded"; like a man who has no mirror, you do not know what your own face is like, you are, as it were, to one side, at a distance from yourself, indifferent and somewhat hostile, an icy void, without light or shade. All the tiny tentacles that constantly stretch out toward the nearby partner, that cling to him, become detached, right themselves, slacken, collide, then come together again, here, like organs that are no longer used, become atrophied and disappear; the subtle, precise movements, the skillful attractions and feigned withdrawals are now reduced to so many blind, disordered jerks, the monotonous starts of a trapped animal; that malleability, or that suggestibility, which had been a furtive, avid caress, has become a docility of inert things, desperate

48

passivity in the face of "an unavoidable fate";
death itself, to which people submit without re-
sisting, because already, for a long time, they
have been nothing but "dead matter," has lost
its nature of unique tragedy; assassination is no
longer the ultimate embrace, nor even the ultimate break, it is only part of a customary and
minutely ordered ritual, at once slightly sicken-
ing and a bit ludicrous, performed by stilted,
clean-shaven "gentlemen," in frock coats and
top hats, filled with delicate, icy courtesy, who
indulge in a lengthy exchange of "polite phrases
to settle questions of precedence," a ritual in
which the victim does his best to participate,
until finally, under the gaze of "gentlemen bend-
ing close to his face, observing him, cheek to
cheek," he dies, slaughtered: "like a dog!"

With the divinatory powers peculiar to certain geniuses, the same that made Dostoievski
foresee the fraternal impulse of the Russian
people and their unusual destiny, Kafka, who
was Jewish, and lived in the shadow of the German nation, foretold the fate that awaited his
people, and understood certain fundamental
features of the German character that were to
lead the Germans to conceive and carry out a
unique experiment: this consisted of yellow

satinette stars distributed upon receipt of two coupons cut from the textile ration-card; of crematoria on which hung large posters giving the name and address of the sanitary firm that had built the model; and of gas chambers in which two thousand naked bodies (as in *The Trial*, their clothes had previously been "carefully folded and put aside") writhed under the gaze of well-girthed, booted and decorated gentlemen, sent on a mission of inspection, who watched them through a glass-covered orifice to which they approached, each in turn, respecting precedence and exchanging polite phrases.

Beyond these furthermost limits, to which Kafka did not follow them, but to which he had the superhuman courage to precede them, all feeling disappears, even contempt and hatred; there remains only vast, empty stupefaction, definitive, total don't-understand.

To remain at the point where he left off, or to attempt to go on from there, are equally impossible. Those who live in a world of human beings can only retrace their steps.

Temps Modernes
October, 1947.

The Age of

Suspicion

Although critics may prefer, like good peda-
gogues, to appear not to notice anything and, on
the other hand, seize every opportunity to pro-
claim, as though announcing a fundamental
truth, that the novel, unless they are very much
mistaken, is and always will be, first and fore-
most, "a story in which characters move and have
their being," that no novelist is worthy of the
name unless he is able to "believe in" his characters, which is what makes it possible for him to
"infuse life" into them and give them "fictional
relief"; although they may continue to lavish

praise on novelists who, like Balzac or Flaubert, succeed in making their hero "stand out," thus adding one more "unforgettable" figure to the unforgettable figures with which so many famous novelists have already peopled our world; although they may dangle before young writers the mirage of exquisite rewards that are supposed to await those whose faith is greatest: that moment, familiar to a few "real novelists," when the character, by virtue of the intensity of the author's belief and interest in him, actuated by some mysterious fluid, as in table-rapping, suddenly starts to move of his own momentum, and takes in tow the delighted creator who has only to let himself be guided, in his turn, by his creature; finally, however sternly critics may add threat to promise, warning novelists that if they are not vigilant, their best-armed rival, the cinema, will one day wrest the scepter from their unworthy hands—it is of no avail. Neither reproaches nor encouragements are able to revive a faith that is waning.

And, according to all appearances, not only has the novelist practically ceased to believe in his characters, but the reader, too, is unable to believe in them; with the result that the characters, having lost the twofold support that the novelist's and the reader's faith afforded them, and which permitted them to stand upright with the burden of the entire story resting on their broad shoulders, may now be seen to vacillate and fall apart.

Since the happy days of Eugénie Grandet when, at the height of his power, the character occupied the place of honor between reader and novelist, the object of their common devotion, like the Saints between the donors in primitive paintings, he has continued to lose, one after the other, his attributes and prerogatives.

At that time he was richly endowed with every asset, the recipient of every attention; he lacked for nothing, from the silver buckles on his breeches to the veined wart on the end of his nose. Since then he has lost everything: his ancestors, his carefully built house, filled from cellar to garret with a variety of objects, down to the tiniest gewgaw, his sources of income and his estates, his clothes, his body, his face. Particularly, however, has he lost that most precious of all possessions, his personality—which belonged to him alone—and frequently, even his name.

Today, a constantly rising tide has been flooding us with literary works that still claim to be novels and in which a being devoid of outline, indefinable, intangible and invisible, an anonymous "I," who is at once all and nothing, and who as often as not is but the reflection of the author himself, has usurped the rôle of the hero, occupying the place of honor. The other characters, being deprived of their own existence, are reduced to the status of visions, dreams, nightmares, illusions, reflections, quiddities or dependents of this all-powerful "I."

Our minds might be set at rest, if we could impute this method of procedure to an egocentricity peculiar to adolescence, to the timidity or inexperience of the beginner. As it happens, however, this youthful malady has attacked some of the most important works of our time (from *Remembrance of Things Past* and *Marshlands,* to the *Miracle de la Rose,* not to mention the *Notebook of Malte Laurids Brigge, Journey to the End of the Night* and *Nausea;* in other words, works in which the authors have given immediate proof of very evident mastery and rare forcefulness.

What is revealed, in fact, by the present evolution of the character in fiction is just the opposite of regression to an infantile state.

It shows, on the part of both author and reader, an unusually sophisticated state of mind. For not only are they both wary of the character, but through him, they are wary of each other. He had been their meeting ground, the solid base from which they could take off in a common effort toward new experiments and new discoveries. He has now become the converging point of their mutual distrust, the devastated ground on which they confront each other. And if we examine his present situation, we are tempted to conclude that it furnishes a perfect illustration of Stendhal's statement that "the genius of suspicion has appeared on the scene." We have now entered upon an age of suspicion.

To begin with, today's reader is suspicious of what the author's imagination has to offer him. "There is nobody left," Jacques Tournier complains, "who is willing to admit that he invents. The only thing that matters is the document, which must be precise, dated, proven, authentic. Works of the imagination are banned, because they are invented . . . (The public), in order to believe what it is told, must be convinced that it is not being 'taken in.' All that counts now is the "true fact . . ."*

* *La Table Ronde,* Paris, January, 1948, p. 145.

But Tournier should not be so bitter. This predilection for "true facts" which, at heart, we all share, does not indicate a timorous, sedate mind, forever ready to crush under the weight of "sound reality" all daring experiment, all impulse toward evasion. On the contrary, we must do the reader the justice of admitting that he needs little coaxing to follow the writer along new paths. He has never really balked before the perspective of effort, and when he agreed to examine with minute attention each detail of Père Grandet's dress and each object in his house, to evaluate his poplar trees and vineyards and supervise his stock-market transactions, it was not because of a liking for sound reality, nor from a need to cuddle down snugly in the nest of a familiar world, whose contours inspired confidence. He knew well where he was being taken. Also, that it would not be plain sailing.

Something unwonted, violent, lay beneath these everyday appearances. Every gesture of the character was a reminder of some aspect of this fact, the most insignificant bauble reflected some facet of it. It was this that had to be brought out, explored to the very limit, investigated in its most secret recesses. Here was a compact, absolutely fresh subject-matter that required effort and fanned the passion for experimental research. Consciousness of this effort and of the validity of this research justified the cocksureness with which the author, indifferent as to whether or not he was trying the reader's patience, forced him to participate in prying housewifely inspections, to make computations that would do honor to a bank clerk or appraisals worthy of an auctioneer. It also justified the reader's tractability. They both realized that here was to be found what, at the time, was their chief concern. Here and nowhere else: as inseparable from the object as the color yellow from the lemon in a Chardin canvas—or, in a Veronese, the color blue from the sky. Just as the color yellow *was* the lemon and the color blue was the sky, and they were inconceivable one without the other, avarice *was* Père Grandet; it was his entire substance, it filled him to the very brim and, at the same time, owed its own form and vigor to him.

The stronger the framework, the better constructed and more richly ornamented the object, the richer and more delicately shaded was the subject matter.

Is it any fault of the reader if, since then, this

same subject matter has taken on the mushy consistency and general insipidness of over-chewed food, and the object containing it the flat appearance of painted scenery?

The sense of life to which, in the long run, all art harks back (the "intensity of life" that undoubtedly, as Gide said, "is what gives things their value"), has deserted these erstwhile promising forms and betaken itself elsewhere. By virtue of the ceaseless movement which tends to bring it ever nearer to the mobile point where, at a given moment, experiment and the peak of effort meet, it has broken through the earlier novel form and forsaken, one by one, all the old, useless accessories. Today, warts and waistcoats, characters and plots, may offer the most infinite variety without revealing anything other than a reality, the slightest particle of which we are familiar with already, from having been over and over it, in every direction. Instead of inciting the reader, as in Balzac's time, to attain to a truth whose conquest denotes hard-won struggle, all these accessories now appear to him to constitute but a dangerous concession to his inclination toward laziness—as well as to that of the author—or to his fear of change. The swiftest glance about him, the most fleeting contact, tell him more than all these external appearances, the sole aim of which is to give a semblance of likelihood to the characters. He has only to dip into the huge stock, which as a result of his own experience is constantly increasing, to compensate for what is lacking in these tiresome descriptions.

As regards the character, he realizes that it is nothing other than a crude label which he himself makes use of, without real conviction and by way of convenience, for the purpose of orienting, very approximately, his own behavior. So he is wary of the abrupt, spectacular types of action that model the character with a few resounding whacks; he is also wary of plot, which winds itself around the character like wrappings, giving it, along with an appearance of cohesiveness and life, mummy-like stiffness.

In fact, Tournier is right; the reader has grown wary of practically everything. The reason being that, for some time now, he has been learning about too many things, and he is unable to forget entirely all he has learned.

What he has learned is a matter of such common knowledge that there is no need to go into it here. He has made the acquaintance of Joyce, Proust and Freud; the trickle, imperceptible from without, of the interior monologue; the infinitely profuse growth of the psychological world and the vast, as yet almost unexplored regions of the unconscious. He has watched the watertight partitions that used to separate the characters from one another give way, and the hero become an arbitrary limitation, a conventional figure cut from the common woof that each of us contains in its entirety, and which captures and holds within its meshes the entire universe. Like the surgeon who eyes the exact spot on which his greatest effort is to be concentrated, isolating it from the rest of the sleeping body, he has been led to center all his attention and curiosity on some new psychological state, forgetting meanwhile the motionless character, who serves as its chance prop. He has seen time cease to be the swift stream that carried the plot forward, and become a stagnant pool at the bottom of which a slow, subtle decomposition is in progress; he has seen our actions lose their usual motives and accepted meanings, he has witnessed the appearance of hitherto unknown sentiments and seen those that were most familiar change both in aspect and name.

In fact, he has learned so much and learned it so well, that he has begun to doubt whether the novelist's artificially constructed object is capable of secreting the wealth of the real object. And since writers of the objective school insist that it is useless to attempt to reproduce the infinite complexity of life, and that it is up to the reader to draw on his own resources, using the instruments of investigation he already possesses to wrest its mystery from the impenetrable object they present to him, he prefers to confine his efforts to certainties, and goes in for facts.

The "true fact" has indeed an indubitable advantage over the invented tale. To begin with, that of being true. This is the source of its strength of conviction and forcefulness, of its noble indifference to ridicule and bad taste, and also of a certain quiet daring, a certain offhandedness, that allow it to break through the confining limitations in which a regard for likelihood imprisons the boldest of novelists, and to extend far afield the frontiers of reality. It allows us to attain to unknown regions into which no writer would have dared venture, and brings us, with one leap, to the edge of the "abyss."

Where is the invented story that could compete with that of Gide's *Séquestrée de Poitiers,* or with those of the concentration camps, or the Battle of Stalingrad? And how many novels, how many characters, situations and plots would be needed to furnish the reader with a subject matter equal in richness and subtlety to that offered for our curiosity and reflection by almost any well-constructed monograph?

It is, therefore, for very wholesome reasons that today's reader prefers accounts of actual experiences (or at least having the reassuring appearance of such) to the novel. Nor, as might be supposed, does the recent vogue of what, in France, is referred to as the "American" novel give the lie to this preference. On the contrary, it confirms it. This particular literature which, for the very reasons just mentioned, is looked down upon by many cultivated American readers, by transporting the French reader into a foreign universe in which he had no foothold, lulled his wariness, aroused in him the kind of credulous curiosity that travel books inspire, and gave him a delightful impression of escape into an unknown world. Now that he has more or less assimilated these exotic foods—which, despite their richness and variety, turned out to be much less tonic than had been supposed— the French reader, as well, is no longer interested.

It goes without saying that all these attitudes with regard to the novel are all the more familiar to the author who, being himself a reader, and often a very perceptive one, has also experienced them.

The result is that when he starts to tell a story and says to himself that he must make up his mind to write down for the mocking eyes of the reader, "The Marquise went out at five o'clock," he hesitates, he hasn't the heart, he simply can't bring himself to do it.

And if, after taking his courage in hand, he decides not to give the Marquise the considerate attention demanded by tradition, but to write only of what interests him today, he realizes that the impersonal tone, which is so well adapted to the needs of the old-style novel, is not suitable for conveying the complex, tenuous states that he is attempting to portray; the fact being that these states resemble certain phenomena of modern physics, which are so delicate and minute that even a ray of light falling on them disturbs and deforms them. Consequently, whenever the novelist seeks to describe them without revealing his own presence, he seems to hear the reader, like a child whose mother is reading him his first story, stop and ask: "Who said that?"

A story told in the first person satisfies the legitimate scruples of the author. In addition, it has the appearance, at least, of real experience and authenticity, which impresses the reader and dispels his mistrust.

For nobody today is entirely misled by the convenient procedure that consists, for the novelist, in parsimoniously apportioning bits of himself, which he invests with a certain likelihood by dividing them, necessarily somewhat at random (if they have been taken from a cross-section performed at a certain depth, they are identical with everyone) among his characters. By a process of decortication, the reader then removes these bits and places them, as in a game of lotto, in corresponding compartments he has discovered in himself.

Today, everybody is well aware, without being told, that *"la Bovary—c'est moi."** And

* From Flaubert's correspondence.

since the important thing now, rather than to extend indefinitely the list of literary types, is to show the co-existence of contradictory emotions and to reproduce as closely as possible the wealth and complexity of the world of the psyche, the writer, in all honesty, writes about himself.

But that's not all. However strange it may seem, this same writer, who is awed by the reader's growing perspicacity and wariness, is, himself, becoming more and more wary of the reader.

For even the most experienced reader, if left to his own devices, tends to create types; he simply can't resist it.

He does it, in fact—in the same way as the novelist, once he has begun to relax—without even noticing that he is doing it, for the convenience of everyday life and as a result of long practice. Like Pavlov's dog, in whom the tinkle of a bell stimulates the secretion of saliva, he creates characters at the slightest possible suggestion. As in the game of "statues," each one he touches turns to stone. They merely serve to swell in his memory the vast collection of inanimate figures to which, day in, day out, he is constantly adding and which, since he first learned to read, has been regularly growing as a result of the countless novels he has absorbed.

But, as has already been demonstrated, the character as conceived in the old-style novel (along with the entire old-style mechanism that was used to make him stand out) does not succeed in containing the psychological reality of today. Instead of revealing it—as used to be the case—he makes it disappear.

So that, as a result of an evolution similar to that in painting—albeit far less bold, less rapid, and interrupted by long pauses and retreats—the psychological element, like the pictorial element, is beginning to free itself imperceptibly from the object of which it was an integral part. It is tending to become self-sufficient and, in so far as possible, to do without exterior support. The novelist's entire experimental effort is concentrated on this one point, as is also the reader's entire effort of attention.

The reader, therefore, must be kept from trying to do two things at one time. And since what the characters gain in the way of facile vitality and plausibility is balanced by a loss of fundamental truth in the psychological states for which they serve as props, he must be kept from allowing his attention to wander or to be absorbed by the characters. For this, he must be deprived as much as possible of all indications which, in spite of himself, and as a result of a natural leaning, he seizes upon in order to create illusions.

This is why the character today is reduced to a shadow of his former self. Only reluctantly does the novelist endow him with attributes that could make him too easily distinguishable: his physical aspect, gestures, actions, sensations, everyday emotions, studied and understood for so long, which contribute to giving him, at the cost of so little effort, an appearance of life, and present such a convenient hold for the reader.* Even a name, which is an absolutely necessary feature of his accoutrement, is a source of embarrassment to the novelist. Gide avoids use of the patronymic for his characters, for the reason that it risks situating them at once in a world too similar to that of the reader, and his preference

* "Not once," wrote Proust, "does one of my characters shut a window, wash his hands, put on his overcoat, utter a phrase of introduction. If there is anything at all new about the book, this would be it! . . ." (Letter to Robert Dreyfus).

is given to unusual forenames. Kafka's hero has for his entire name an initial only (that of Kafka himself); Joyce designates by the initials, H.C.E., of multiple interpretations, the protean hero of *Finnegans Wake*. And it would be most unfair to Faulkner's bold and very worthwhile experiments, which are so revealing of the problem of the present-day novelist, if we were to attribute to a perverse and childish desire to mystify the reader, the method used by him in *The Sound and the Fury* which consists in giving the same forename to two different characters.* This first name, which he shunts back and forth from one character to the other, under the annoyed eye of the reader, like a lump of sugar under the nose of a dog, forces the reader to be constantly on the alert. Instead of letting himself be guided by the signposts with which everyday custom flatters his laziness and haste, he is obliged, in order to identify the characters, to recognize them at once, like the author himself, from the inside, and thanks to indications that are only revealed to him if, having renounced his love of comfort, he is willing to

* Quentin is the first name of both the uncle and the niece; Caddy, that of the mother and the daughter.

plunge into them as deeply as the author, whose vision he makes his own.

Indeed, the whole problem is here: to dispossess the reader and entice him, at all costs, into the author's territory. To achieve this, the device that consists in referring to the leading character as "I" constitutes a means that is both efficacious and simple and, doubtless for this reason, is frequently employed.

Suddenly the reader is on the inside, exactly where the author is, at a depth where nothing remains of the convenient landmarks with which he constructs the characters. He is immersed and held under the surface until the end, in a substance as anonymous as blood, a magma without name or contours. If he succeeds in finding his way, it is thanks to stakes that the author has planted for purposes of his own orientation. No reminiscences of the reader's world, no conventional concern for cohesion or likelihood, distract his attention or curb his effort. Like the author, the only barriers he encounters are those that are either inherent to all experiments of this kind or peculiar to the author's vision.

As for the secondary characters, they are deprived of all autonomous existence and reduced to mere excrescences, quiddities, experiments or dreams of the "I," with whom the author identifies himself. At the same time, this "I," not being the novelist, need not be concerned with creating a universe in which the reader will feel too much at home, nor with giving the characters the proportions and dimensions required to confer upon them their rather dangerous "resemblance." His obsessed, maniacal or visionary eye may seize upon them at will, abandon them, stretch them in a single direction, compress, enlarge, flatten or reduce them to dust, to force them to yield the new reality he is striving to find.

In the same way, the modern painter—and in this connection it might be said that, since Impressionism, all pictures have been painted in the first person—wrests the object from the universe of the spectator and deforms it in order to isolate its pictorial content.

Thus, in a movement analogous to that of painting, the novel, which only a stubborn adherence to obsolete techniques places in the position of a minor art, pursues with means that are uniquely its own a path which can only be its own; it leaves to the other arts—and, in particular, to the cinema—everything that does not actually belong to it. In the same way that photography occupies and fructifies the fields abandoned by painting, the cinema garners and perfects what is left by the novel.

The reader, instead of demanding of the novel what every good novel has more than often refused him, i.e., light entertainment, can satisfy at the cinema, without effort and without needless loss of time, his taste for "live" characters and stories.

However, the cinema too would appear to be threatened. It too is infected by the "suspicion" from which the novel suffers. Otherwise, how may we explain the uneasiness which, after that of the novelist, is now being evidenced by certain "advanced" directors who, because they feel obliged to make films in the first person, have introduced the eye of a witness and the voice of a narrator?

As for the novel, before it has even exhausted all the advantages offered by the story told in the first person, or reached the end of the blind alley into which all techniques necessarily lead, it has grown impatient and, in order to emerge from its present difficulties, is looking about for other ways out.

Suspicion, which is by way of destroying the

character and the entire outmoded mechanism that guaranteed its force, is one of the morbid reactions by which an organism defends itself and seeks another equilibrium. It forces the novelist to fulfill what Arnold Toynbee, recalling Flaubert's teaching, has called "his deepest obligation: that of discovering what is new," and keeps him from committing "his most serious crime: that of repeating the discoveries of his predecessors."

Temps Modernes
February, 1950.

Conversation

and

Sub-conversation

Who today would dream of taking seriously, or even reading, the articles that Virginia Woolf wrote, shortly after the First World War, on the art of the novel? Their naïve confidence, their innocence of another age, would only elicit a smile. "It is difficult," she wrote with enviable candor, "not to take it for granted that the modern practice of the art is somehow an improvement upon the old." . . . The tools used by classical writers were "simple," their materials were "primitive," and their masterpieces, in her opinion, had "an air of simplicity." "But compare their opportunities with ours!" she said. And she added proudly that, "for the moderns," the point of interest would "very likely lie in the dark places of psychology."

No doubt she had much to excuse her: *Ulysses* had just appeared. *In a Budding Grove* was about to receive the Goncourt Prize. She herself was working on *Mrs. Dalloway*. Quite obviously, she lacked perspective.

But for most people, the works of Joyce and Proust already rise up in the distance like witnesses of a past epoch, and the day will soon come when no one will visit these historical monuments otherwise than with a guide, along with groups of school children, in respectful silence and somewhat dreary admiration. For several years now interest in "the dark places of psychology" has waned. This twilight zone in which, hardly thirty years ago, we thought we saw the gleam of real treasures, has yielded us very little, and we are obliged to acknowledge that, when all is said and done, this exploration, however bold and well carried out it may have been, however extensive and with whatever elaborate means, has ended in disappointment. The most impatient and most daring among the novelists were not long in declaring that the game was not worth the candle, and that they preferred to turn their efforts in another direction. The word "psychology" is one that no present-day writer can hear spoken with regard to himself without casting his eyes to the ground and blushing. It has something slightly ridiculous, antiquated, cerebral, limited, not to say pretentiously silly about it. Intelligent people, all progressive minds to whom an imprudent writer would dare admit his secret hankering for the "dark places of psychology"—but who would dare to do so?—would undoubtedly reply with pitying surprise: "Indeed! so you still believe in all that? . . ." Since the appearance of the "American novel" and the profound, blinding truths with which the literature of the absurd has continued to swamp us, there are not many left who believe in it. All Joyce obtained from those dark depths was an uninterrupted flow of words. As for Proust, however doggedly he may have separated into minute fragments the intangible matter that he brought up from the subsoil of his characters, in the hope of extracting from it some indefinable, anonymous substance which would enter into the composition of all humanity, the reader has hardly closed the book before, through an irresistible movement of attraction, all these particles begin to cling to one another and amalgamate into a coherent whole with clear outlines, in which the practiced eye of the reader immediately recognizes a rich man of the world in love with a kept woman, a prominent, awkward, gullible doctor, a parvenue bourgeoise or a snobbish "great lady," all of whom will soon take their places in the vast collection of fictitious characters that people his imaginary museum.

What enormous pains to achieve results that, without contortions and without hairsplitting, are obtained, shall we say, by Hemingway. And this being the case, if he handles them with equal felicity, why object to the fact that he uses the same tools that served Tolstoy in such good stead?

But there's no question of Tolstoy! Today, eighteenth- and even seventeenth-century writers are constantly being held up to us as models. And should some die-hard, at the risk of his life, continue to want to explore gropingly the "dark places," he is immediately referred back to the *Princess of Cleve* and *Adolph*. He should read the classics a bit! Would he for a moment claim to penetrate farther than they did into the depths of the soul, or with such ease and grace, with so keen, so light a touch?

Indeed, as soon as a writer renounces the legacy of those whom, thirty years ago, Virginia Woolf called "moderns" and, disdaining the liberties (the "facilities," he would say) that they conquered, succeeds in capturing a few reactions of the soul couched in the pure, simple, elegant lines that characterize the classical style, he is praised to the skies. With what alacrity, what generosity, people exert themselves to discover an abundance of inexpressible sentiments beneath his reticence and silence, to see reserve and contained strength in the prudence and abstinence that are forced upon him by constant concern for maintaining the "figure" of his style.

However, the unfortunate die-hard who, being unconcerned by the indifference and reproval awaiting him, persists nevertheless in digging in these dark regions, in the hope of extracting from them a few particles of an unknown substance, does not, for all that, enjoy the peace of mind that his independence and disinterestedness should ensure him.

Frequently, doubts and scruples slacken his endeavors. For where is he to find and be able to examine these secret recesses that attract him, if not in himself, or in the persons in his immediate circle whom he feels he knows well and whom he imagines he resembles? And the tiny, evanescent movements they conceal blossom out preferably in immobility and withdrawal. The din of actions accomplished in broad daylight either drowns or checks them.

But he is well aware, as he observes himself and his fellow-creatures from his inner sanctum, steeping in the protective liquid of his tightly sealed little jar, that, on the outside, very important things (perhaps—and he tells himself this with anguish—the only really important things) are happening: men who are probably very different from him, as well as from his family and friends, men who have other fish to fry than to hover solicitously over their innermost quakings, and in whom, moreover, it would seem that deep suffering, deep, simple joys, powerful, very evident needs must quell these very subtle tremors, men toward whom he feels drawn, whom, often, he admires, are acting and struggling; and he knows that, to be at peace with his conscience and meet the requirements of his time, it is with them and not with himself or those like him that he should be concerned.

But if, having torn himself away from his jar, he attempts to turn his attention toward these men and make them come to life in his books, he is assailed by fresh misgivings. His eyes, having become accustomed to semi-darkness, are dazzled by the garish light of the outside. As a result of examining only the tiny space around him, of staring lengthily at one spot, they have become magnifying lenses that are incapable of taking in vast expanses at one time. Long maceration in his jar has made him lose his innocent freshness. He has seen how difficult it was, when he examined closely some tiny recess in himself, to make an inventory of all the things to be found there: not of any great importance, he is well aware, more than often disappointing, but concerning which a rapid examination, made from a distance, would never have permitted him even to suspect their existence. He consequently has the impression of not seeing these men from the outside clearly. Their actions, which he respects and admires, seem to him to be like very wide-mesh nets: they let slip through their large holes all this turbid, teeming matter to which he has grown accustomed, and he is unable to break himself of the habit of looking for the living substance, for him the only living substance; also, he is obliged to admit that he sees nothing in what they bring back but large empty carcasses. These men whom he would so like to know and make known, when he tries to show them moving about in the blinding light of day, seem to him to be nothing but well-made dolls, intended for the amusement of children.

Furthermore, if it is a matter of showing characters from the outside, devoid of all swarmings and secret tremors, and of recounting their actions and the events that compose their story, of telling stories about them, as he is so often incited to do (isn't this, people continually tell him, the gift that best characterizes the real writer?), the cinema director, who disposes of means of expression that are far better suited to this purpose and much more powerful than his own, succeeds, with less fatigue and loss of time for the spectator, in easily surpassing him. And when it comes to describing men's sufferings and struggles plausibly, to making known all the frequently monstrous, almost unbelievable iniquities that are committed, the journalist possesses the immense advantage over him of being able to give to the facts he reports—however unlikely they may seem—that look of authenticity which, alone, is capable of compelling the reader's credence.

Lacking encouragement, lacking confidence, with a frequently painful sense of guilt and boredom, he had no alternative, therefore, but to return to himself. But here, although he has plunged once more into his jar after this evasion, which is more than often imaginary— he is usually far too distrustful and discouraged in advance to venture outside—it would be painting far too black a picture of his situation, if we did not say that, to his own astonishment and pretty rarely at that, he occasionally experiences moments of satisfaction and hope.

One fine day he hears that even out yonder, on the outside, not in those gloomy, solitary regions in which he is groping about, and into which the little company of moderns had once ventured, but in the rich, eternally fertile, well-populated and carefully cultivated lands where

tradition continues to blossom in the sun, people have finally noticed that, after all, something is happening. Novelists whom nobody
would ever accuse of making revolutionary
claims are forced to recognize certain changes.
One of the best contemporary English novelists,
Henry Green, has pointed out that the center
of gravity of the novel has moved, that more
and more importance is being given to dialogue. "Today," he writes, "it is the best way
to give the reader real life." And he even pre-
dicts that it will be "the principal support of
the novel for a long time to come."

In the silence that surrounds him, this simple
statement is an olive branch for our die-hard.
It makes him take heart immediately. It even
revives his wildest dreams. No doubt, the explanation Mr. Green gives of this change risks
destroying all the promise contained in his remark: it is probably, he adds, because "nowa-
days people have stopped writing letters. Instead, they use the telephone." It is not to be
wondered at then that, in their turn, characters in fiction should have become so talkative.

But this explanation is disappointing in appearance only. It should not be forgotten that

Mr. Green is English, and it is well known that reserve often incites his countrymen to adopt a tone of playful simplicity when speaking of serious matters. Or perhaps it is a dash of humor. Perhaps, too, after making this bold statement, Henry Green experienced a certain fear: if he were to carry his investigation too far, where would it not lead him? Might he not eventually come to ask himself if this single indication of his were not a sign of profound disturbances that could lead to re-examination of the entire traditional structure of the novel? Might he not end by claiming that contemporary novel forms are cracking on all sides, and thus instigate, even invite, new techniques adapted to new forms? But the words "new forms" and "techniques" are even more immodest and embarrassing to pronounce than the word "psychology" itself. They result immediately in your being accused of presumption and bumptiousness, and arouse, in both critics and readers, a feeling of mistrust and annoyance. It is consequently more proper and more prudent to limit oneself to mention of the telephone.

But however great our novelist's fear of appearing to yield to an enthusiasm that is suspect, he cannot be content with this explanation. For it is above all when he must make his characters speak that it seems to him that something is changing, and that it appears most difficult to avail himself of the methods that have been in current usage thus far. Between Henry Green's observation and his own impressions and reluctance there must be something more than mere coincidence. And from then on, everything changes: the confusion he senses is apparently not, as people tell him, and as he himself in his moments of depression is liable to think, that of senility, but of growth; his endeavors would seem to make him go forward in the direction of a vast general movement. And all the arguments used against those whom Virginia Woolf called moderns could be turned to their advantage.

But, people say, it is not possible to repeat what they did. Their techniques, in the hands of those who attempt to use them today, immediately become a device, whereas the traditional novel retains eternal youth. Without having to undergo any appreciable changes, its generous, supple forms continue to adapt themselves to all the new stories, all the new characters and new conflicts that appear in the societies that succeed one another, and it is in the novelty of these characters and conflicts that the principal interest and only valid renewal of the novel lie.

And it is true that we cannot repeat what Joyce or Proust did, even though Stendhal and Tolstoy are repeated every day to everybody's satisfaction. But isn't this, first of all, because the moderns displaced the essential interest of the novel? For them it no longer lies in the enumeration of situations and characters, or in the portrayal of manners and customs, but in the revelation of a new psychological subject matter. Indeed, it is the discovery, if only of a few particles of this subject matter, which is an anonymous one, to be found in all men and in all societies, that constituted for them and continues to constitute for their successors, genuine renewal. To re-work after them this same material and, consequently, to use their methods without changing them in any way, would be quite as absurd as for supporters of the traditional novel to re-write with the same characters, the same plot and the same style, *The Red and the Black* or *War and Peace*.

On the other hand, the techniques used today

with occasionally still excellent results by advocates of tradition, techniques invented by novelists of another day to explore the unknown material that fell within their range of vision, and which were perfectly adapted to this purpose, these techniques have ended by constituting a very strong, coherent system of conventions which is well constructed and entirely closed; a universe that has its own laws and is self-sufficient. Through force of habit, by virtue of the authority conferred upon it, and because of the great works it has engendered, it has become a second nature. It has assumed a necessary, an eternal aspect. So much so that, today still, those persons, whether writers or readers, who have been the most disturbed by all the upheavals that have been taking place for some time now outside its thick walls, as soon as they enter within them, docilely allow themselves to be confined there; they very soon feel quite at home, accept all limitations, conform to all restraints, and abandon all dreams of escape.

But by freeing themselves of its fetters, the moderns, who sought to tear themselves as well as their readers away from this system, lost the protection and security it offered. And the reader, being deprived of all his accustomed stakes and landmarks, removed from all authority, suddenly faced with an unknown substance, bewildered and distrustful, instead of blindly letting himself go, as he so loves to do, was obliged constantly to confront what was shown him with what he could see for himself.

Just in passing, he must have been extremely surprised by the opacity of the fictional conventions that had succeeded in concealing for so long what should have been obvious to all eyes. But once he had taken a good look and arrived at an independent judgment, he was unable to stop there. At the same time that they had awakened his powers of penetration, the moderns had awakened his critical faculties and whetted his curiosity.

He wanted to look even further or, if one prefers, even closer. And he was not long in perceiving what is hidden beneath the interior monologue: an immense profusion of sensations, images, sentiments, memories, impulses, little larval actions that no inner language can convey, that jostle one another on the threshold of consciousness, gather together in compact groups and loom up all of a sudden, then immediately fall apart, combine otherwise and reappear in new forms; while unwinding inside us, like the ribbon that comes clattering from a telescriptor slot, is an uninterrupted flow of words.

With regard to Proust, it is true that these groups composed of sensations, images, sentiments and memories which, when traversing or skirting the thin curtain of the interior monologue, suddenly become visible from the outside, in an apparently insignificant word, a mere intonation or a glance, are precisely what he took such pains to study. But however paradoxical this may seem to those who, today, still reproach him for his extreme minutiae, to us it appears already as though he had observed them from a great distance, after they had run their course, in repose and, as it were, congealed in memory. He tried to describe their respective positions as though they were stars in a motionless sky. He considered them as a sequence of causes and effects which he sought to explain. He rarely—not to say never—tried to relive them and make them relive for the reader in the present, while they were forming and developing, like so many tiny dramas, each one of which has its adventures, its mystery and its unforeseeable ending.

It was doubtless this that prompted Gide to say that he had collected the raw material for a great work rather than achieved the work itself, and that brought upon him the serious reproach still made today by his opponents, of having gone in for "analysis," that is to say, in the most original parts of his work, of having incited the reader to use his own intelligence, instead of giving him the sensation of reliving an experience, of accomplishing certain actions himself, without knowing too well what he is doing or where he is going—which always was and still is in the very nature of any work of fiction.

But isn't this like reproaching Christopher Columbus with not having constructed the port of New York?

Those who have followed him and who have wanted to try to make these subterranean actions relive for the reader as they unfold, have met with certain difficulties. Because these inner dramas composed of attacks, triumphs, recoils, defeats, caresses, bites, rapes, murders, generous renunciations or humble submissions, all have one thing in common: they cannot do without a partner.

Often it is an imaginary partner who emerges from out our past experiences, or from our day-dreams, and the scenes of love or combat between us, by virtue of their wealth of adventure, the freedom with which they unfold and what they reveal concerning our least apparent inner structure, can constitute very valuable fictional material.

It remains nonetheless true that the essential feature of these dramas is constituted by an actual partner.

For this flesh-and-blood partner is constantly nurturing and renewing our stock of experiences. He is pre-eminently the catalyzer, the stimulant, thanks to whom these movements are set in motion, the obstacle that gives them cohesion, that keeps them from growing soft from ease and gratuitousness, or from going round and round in circles in the monotonous indigence of ruminating on one thing. He is the threat, the real danger as well as the prey that brings out their alertness and their suppleness, the mysterious element whose unforeseeable reactions, by making them continually start up again and evolve toward an unknown goal, accentuate their dramatic nature.

But at the same time that, in order to attain to this partner, they rise up from our darkest recesses toward the light of day, a certain fear forces them back toward the shadow. They make us think of the little gray insects that hide in damp holes. They are abashed and prudent. The slightest look makes them flee. To blossom out they must have anonymity and impunity.

They consequently hardly show themselves in the form of actions. For actions do indeed develop in the open, in the garish light of day, and the tiniest of them, compared with these delicate, minute inner movements, appear to be gross and violent: they immediately attract attention. All their forms have long since been examined and classified; they are subject to strict rules, to very frequent inspection. Finally, very obvious, well-known, frank motives, thick, perfectly visible wires make all this enormous, heavy machinery work.[1]

[1] These gross motives, these vast, apparent movements, are usually all that is seen by both writers and readers, who are borne along by the movement of the

But lacking actions, we can use words. And words possess the qualities needed to seize upon, protect and bring out into the open these sub-

---

action and spurred on by the plot in behaviorist novels. They have neither time nor means—not having at their disposal a sufficiently delicate instrument of investigation—to see clearly the more fleeting, subtler movements that these grosser movements may conceal.

Indeed, we can understand the aversion these writers feel for what they call "analysis," which, for them, would consist in pointing out these perfectly visible, frank motives, thus doing the reader's work for him and giving themselves the disagreeable impression of forcing already open doors.

It is nevertheless curious to observe that, to escape the boredom of going round and round in the narrow circle of customary actions, in which they find really nothing much left to be gleaned, seized with the desire natural to all writers to take their readers into unknown regions, and haunted, in spite of everything, by the existence of the "dark places," but still firmly convinced that action by itself can reveal them, they make their characters commit unwonted, monstrous acts which the reader, comfortably settled in his own clear conscience and finding nothing in these criminal acts that corresponds to what he has learned to see in his own conduct, regards with proud, horrified curiosity, then quietly thrusts aside to return to his own affairs, as he does every morning and every evening after reading his newspaper, without the heavy shadow that submerges his own dark places having lifted for a single second.

terranean movements that are at once impatient and afraid.

They have in their favor their suppleness, their freedom, the iridescent richness of their shadings, their transparency or their opaqueness.

Their rapid, abundant flow, with its restless shimmer, allows the more imprudent of them to slip by, to let themselves be borne along and disappear at the slightest sign of danger. But they risk little danger. Their reputation for gratuitousness, lightness, inconsistency—they are, after all, pre-eminently the instruments of frivolous pastimes and games—protects them from suspicion and from minute examination: we are generally content to make purely formal verification of them; they are subject to rather lax regulations; they rarely result in serious sanctions.

Consequently, provided they present a more or less harmless, commonplace appearance, they can be and, in fact, without anyone's taking exception, without the victim's even daring to admit it frankly to himself, they often are the daily, insidious and very effective weapon responsible for countless minor crimes.

For there is nothing to equal the rapidity

with which they attain to the other person at the moment when he is least on his guard, often giving him merely a sensation of disagreeable tickling or slight burning; or the precision with which they enter straight into him at his most secret and most vulnerable points, and lodge in his innermost recesses, without his having the desire, the means or the time to retort. But once they are deposited inside him, they begin to swell, to explode, they give rise around them to waves and eddies which, in turn, come up to the surface and spread out in words. By virtue of this game of actions and reactions that they make possible, they constitute for the novelist a most valuable tool.

And this, no doubt, is why, as Henry Green has noted, characters in fiction have become so talkative.

But this dialogue, which tends more and more, in the modern novel, to take the place left by action, does not adapt itself easily to the forms imposed by the traditional novel. For it is above all the outward continuation of sub-terranean movements which the author—and with him the reader—must make at the same time as the character, from the moment they form until the moment when, having been forced to the surface by their increasing intensity, to reach the other person and protect themselves from exterior dangers, they cloak themselves in the protective capsules of words.

Nothing, therefore, should break the continuity of these movements, and the transformation they undergo should be analogous to that sustained by a ray of light when, as it passes from one sphere into another, it is refracted and inflected.

This being the case, there is really no justification for the heavy indentations and dashes with which we are accustomed to sharply separate dialogue from what precedes it. Even the colon and quotation marks are still too apparent, and it is understandable that certain novelists (for instance, Joyce Cary) should strive to blend dialogue with its context—to the extent that this is possible—by simply marking the separation with a comma followed by a capital.

But even more awkward and hard to defend than indentations, dashes, colons and quotation marks are the monotonous, clumsy: "said Jeanne," "answered Paul," with which dialogue is usually strewn; for contemporary novelists these are becoming more and more what the laws of perspective had become for painters just before Cubism: no longer a necessity, but a cumbersome convention.

Indeed, it is curious to see that, today, those very novelists who refuse to let themselves become what they consider to be needlessly disturbed, and who continue to use the devices of the old-fashioned novel with blithe assurance, seem unable to escape a certain feeling of uneasiness as regards this particular point. It is as though they had lost that certainty of being within their rights, that innocent unawareness that gives to the "said, resumed, replied, retorted, exclaimed etc. . . ." with which Madame de Lafayette or Balzac so brightly studded their dialogues, that look of being securely where they belong, indispensable and perfectly as a matter of course, that makes us accept them without raising an eyebrow, without even noticing it, when we reread these authors today. And compared to them, how self-conscious, anxious and unsure of themselves contemporary novelists seem, when they use these same formulas.

At times—like people who prefer to flaunt and even to accentuate their faults to ward off danger and disarm their critics—they ostentatiously renounce the subterfuges used ingenuously by writers of the old school (which today seem to them to be too gross and too easy, and which consisted in constantly varying their formulas), and expose the monotony and clumsiness of this device by repeating tirelessly, with affected negligence or naïveté, "said Jeanne," "said Paul," "said Jacques," the only result being to fatigue and irritate the reader all the more.

At others, they try to make these unfortunate "said Jeanne," "replied Paul," disappear, by following them, on every occasion, with repetitions of the last words of the dialogue: "No," said Jeanne, "no" or: "It's finished," said Paul, "it's finished." This gives to the words the characters speak a solemn, emotional tone which obviously does not correspond to the author's intention. Then, again, they do away as much as possible with this cumbersome appendix by continually introducing the dialogue in a still more artificial way which we feel does not answer to any inner necessity: Jeanne smiled: "I leave the choice to you," or: Madeleine looked at him: "I was the one who did it."

All these resorts to too apparent subterfuges,

all these embarrassed attitudes, are a source of great cheer to followers of the moderns. They see in them premonitory signs, proof that something is falling apart, that there is filtering insidiously into the minds of the supporters of the traditional novel a doubt as to the merits of their rights, a scruple at entering into possession of their inheritance which, without their realizing it, makes of them, as it were, the privileged classes before revolutions, the agents of future upheavals.

Indeed, it is not by mere chance that it should be at the moment when they use these short, apparently harmless formulas that they feel most ill at ease. For, in a way, these are symbols of the old regime, the point at which the old and the new conceptions of the novel separate most distinctly. They mark the site on which the novelist has always located his characters, that is, at a point as remote from himself as from the reader; there where the players are to be found in a tennis match, while the novelist occupies the place of the umpire perched on his stool, supervising the game and announcing the score to the fans (in this case, the readers) seated on the sidelines.

Neither the novelist nor the readers leave

their seats to play the game themselves, as though they were players.

And this remains true when the character expresses himself in the first person, as soon as he begins to follow his own statements with, "I said," "I cried," "I replied," etc. . . . He shows by this that he himself does not perform, nor does he make his readers perform, the inner movements that prepare the dialogue, from the moment they originate until the moment when they appear externally, but that, keeping himself at a distance, he makes this dialogue start up in the presence of an insufficiently prepared reader whom he is obliged to warn.

Being thus on the outside and at a distance from his characters, the novelist can adopt devices that vary from those of the behaviorists to those of Marcel Proust.

Like the behaviorists, he can make his characters speak without any preparation while he remains at a distance, limiting himself to apparently recording their dialogues and thus giving the impression of allowing them to live lives of their own.

But nothing is more deceptive than this impression.

Because although the little appendix that the

novelist places after their spoken words shows that the author gives his creatures their head, it recalls at the same time that he is keeping a firm hold on the reins. These "said," "continued," etc. . . . that are delicately inserted in the midst of the dialogue, or prolong it harmoniously, are quiet reminders that the author is still present, and that this fictional dialogue, despite its apparent independence, cannot do without him and stand alone in the air, the way theatrical dialogue does; they are the light but strong ties that bind and subject the style and tone of the characters to the style and tone of the author.

As for the famous *intaglio* implications that the supporters of this system think they obtain by giving no explanations, it would be interesting to ask the most experienced and most sensitive among their readers to tell sincerely what they perceive, when left to themselves, beneath the words spoken by the characters. How much do they guess of all those tiny actions that subtend and set the dialogue in motion, giving it its real meaning? Undoubtedly the suppleness, subtlety, variety and abundance of words permit the reader to sense movements beneath them that are more numerous, sharper and more secret than those he can discover beneath actions. We should nevertheless be surprised by the simplicity, the grossness and the approximation of his perceptions.

But it would be a mistake to blame the reader.

Because, to make this dialogue "lifelike" and plausible, these novelists give it the conventional form that it has in everyday life: it consequently reminds the reader too much of the dialogues he himself is accustomed to record hastily, without asking too many questions, without looking for hidden difficulties (he has neither the time nor the means to do so, and this is exactly what the author's work consists of), being content to perceive beneath the spoken words only that which allows him to order his own conduct somehow or other, without lingering morbidly over vague, dubious impressions.

But better still, what the reader discovers beneath these fictional dialogues—however loaded with secret meanings their author may have wanted them to be—is not much compared with what he himself can discover when, as a participant in the game, with all his instincts of defense and attack aroused, excited and on the alert, he observes and listens to those with whom he is talking.

Above all, it is not much compared to what the spectator learns from theatrical dialogue.

Because theatrical dialogue, which needs no props, and during which the author does not constantly make us feel that he is present, ready to lend a hand, this dialogue, which must be self-sufficient and on which everything rests, is denser, tauter, more compact and at a higher tension than fictional dialogue: it makes greater demands on the combined powers of the spectator.

But above all, the actors are there to do most of the work for him. Their entire task consists in recapturing and reproducing within themselves, at the cost of great, prolonged effort, the tiny, complicated inner movements that have propelled the dialogue, that give it weight, distend and tauten it, and, by their gestures, their acting, their intonations, their silences, in communicating these movements to the audience.

Behaviorist novelists, who make abundant use of dialogue, set between brief indications or discreet commentaries, extend the novel dangerously near the domain of the theater, where it is bound to be in a position of inferiority. And by renouncing the means that the novel alone has at its disposal, they renounce what makes it a unique art, or rather, simply an art.

There remains, then, the opposite method, Proust's, or recourse to analysis. This latter one, in any case, has the advantage over the former of maintaining the novel on its own ground, and using means that only the novel affords. It also tends to furnish the reader with what he has a right to expect from a novelist; that is, experience increased not in breadth (this may be had at less cost and more effectively through documents and news reports) but in depth. And above all, it is not conducive, under the cloak of so-called renovations, to an attachment to the past, but looks frankly toward the future.

As regards dialogue, in particular, Proust himself—concerning whom it is no exaggeration to say that, more than any other novelist, he excelled in the very minute, exact, subtle, highly evocative descriptions of the play of features, the glances, the slightest intonations and inflections of voice in his characters, which give the reader almost as much information as actors would with regard to the secret meaning of their words

—is practically never content with simple description, and he rarely leaves the dialogue to the reader's free interpretation. He only does so, in fact, when the apparent meaning of the words spoken exactly covers the hidden meaning. Should there be the slightest discrepancy between the conversation and the sub-conversation, should they not entirely cover each other, he immediately intervenes; at times, before the character speaks, at others, as soon as he has spoken, to show all he sees, explain all he knows; and he leaves no uncertainty except that which he himself is bound to feel, in spite of all his endeavors, his privileged position, the powerful instruments of investigation he has forged.

But these countless, tiny movements which prepare the dialogue are for Proust, from his point of observation, what waves and eddies on a body of water are for a cartographer who is studying a region from the air; he only sees and reproduces the broad, motionless lines that these movements compose, the points at which the lines join, cross or separate; he recognizes among them those that have already been explored, and designates them by their known names: jealousy, snobbishness, fear, modesty, etc. . . . ;

he describes, classifies and names those he has discovered; he seeks to deduce general principles from his observations. On this vast map representing, for the most part, hardly explored regions, which he spreads out before his readers, the latter, their eyes glued to his pointer with all the attention they can summon, try their best to see clearly; and they feel rewarded for their pains every time they succeed in recognizing and following visually to the very end those frequently numerous, long lines, when, like rivers that flow into the sea, they cross, separate and mingle in the mass of the dialogue.

But by appealing to the reader's voluntary attention, to his memory, by continually calling upon his faculties of comprehension and reasoning, this method forgoes at the same time everything upon which the behaviorists, with exaggerated optimism, founded all their hopes: namely, an element of freedom, of what is inexpressible, of mystery, the direct and purely sensory contact with things, which should bring into action all the reader's instinctive faculties, the resources of his unconscious, and his divinatory powers.

Although the results obtained by the behaviorists through appeal to these blind forces are undoubtedly much weaker than their authors are willing to believe—even in those of their works in which the implications are richest and the sub-surface indications deepest—it is nonetheless true that these forces exist and that one of the virtues of a work of fiction is to allow them also to come into play.

And yet, in spite of the rather serious charges that may be brought against analysis, it is difficult to turn from it today without turning one's back on progress.

For it is surely preferable, in spite of all obstacles and possible disappointments, to try to perfect, with a view to adapting it to fresh research, an instrument which, when further perfected by new generations, will permit them to describe more convincingly, with more truth and life, new situations and sentiments, than to fall back upon devices made to seize what today is mere appearance, to tend to strengthen more and more the natural penchant we all have for effects of illusion.

It is therefore permissible to dream—without blinding ourselves to all that separates the dream from its reality—of a technique that might succeed in plunging the reader into the stream of these subterranean dramas of which Proust only had time to obtain a rapid aerial view, and concerning which he observed and reproduced nothing but the broad motionless lines. This technique would give the reader the illusion of repeating these actions himself, in a more clearly aware, more orderly, distinct and forceful manner than he can do in life, without their losing that element of indetermination, of opacity and mystery that one's own actions always have for the one who lives them.

The dialogue, which would be merely the outcome or, at times, one of the phases of these dramas, would then, quite naturally, free itself of the conventions and restraints that were made indispensable by the methods of the traditional novel. And thus, imperceptibly, through a change of rhythm or form, which would espouse and at the same time accentuate his own sensation, the reader would become aware that the action has moved from inside to outside.

The dialogue, having become vibrant and swollen with these movements that propel and subtend it, would be as revealing as theatrical dialogue, however commonplace it might seem in appearance.

All of this, of course, being merely a matter for possible research and hope.

However, these problems, which dialogue poses more and more urgently to all novelists, whether they care to recognize it or not, have been solved, up to a certain point, only in a very different way, by an English writer who is still little known in France, Ivy Compton-Burnett.

The absolutely original solution, which has both distinction and power, that she has found for them, would suffice for her to deserve the position unanimously accorded her by English critics and by a certain portion of the English reading-public; that is, the position of one of the greatest novelists that England has ever had.

Indeed we cannot help admiring the discernment of both critics and public who have been able to see the novelty and importance of a work which, in many respects, is disconcerting.

For nothing could be less timely than the social groups that Ivy Compton-Burnett describes (the wealthy upper middle-class and the petty English nobility during the years 1880 to 1900); nothing could be more limited than the family circle in which her characters move, nothing more outmoded than the descriptions of their appearance, with which she introduces them, or more astonishing than the off-handedness with which she unravels her plots, according to the most conventional methods, and the monotonous obstinacy with which, during forty years of labor, and throughout twenty books, she has posed and solved, in an identical manner, the same problems.

But her books have one absolutely new feature, which is that they are nothing but one long continuation of dialogue. Here again, the author presents them in the traditional manner, holding herself aloof, very ceremoniously aloof, from her characters, and limiting herself as a rule, just as the behaviorists do, to simply reproducing their words and quietly informing the reader, without trying to vary her formulas, by means of the monotonous "said X.," "said Y."

But these dialogues, upon which everything rests, have nothing in common with the short, brisk, lifelike conversations that, reduced to themselves, or accompanied by a few cursory explanations, risk reminding us more and more of the heavily circled little clouds that issue from the mouths of the figures in comic supplement drawings.

These long, stilted sentences, which are at once stiff and sinuous, do not recall any conversations we ever heard. And yet, although they seem strange, they never give an impression of being spurious or gratuitous.

The reason for this is that they are located not in an imaginary place, but in a place that actually exists: somewhere on the fluctuating frontier that separates conversation from sub-conversation. Here the inner movements, of which the dialogue is merely the outcome and, as it were, the furthermost point—usually prudently tipped to allow it to come up to the surface—try to extend their action into the dialogue itself. To resist their constant pressure and contain them, the conversation stiffens, becomes stilted, it adopts a cautious, slackened pace. But it is because of this pressure that it stretches and twists into long sinuous sentences. Now a close, subtle game, which is also a savage game, takes place between the conversation and the sub-conversation.

More often than not, the inside gets the better of it: something keeps cropping out, becoming manifest, disappearing then coming back again; something that continually threatens to make everything explode.

The reader, who has remained intent, on the lookout, as though he were in the shoes of the person to whom the words are directed, mobilizes all his instincts of defense, all his powers of intuition, his memory, his faculties of judgment and reasoning; there is hidden danger in these sweetish sentences, murderous impulses are creeping into affectionate solicitude, an expression of tenderness suddenly distills a subtle venom.

Occasionally, ordinary conversation appears to win the day, when it suppresses the sub-conversation too deeply. Then, often just at the moment when the reader thinks he will finally be able to relax, the author suddenly abandons her silence and intervenes to warn him briefly and without explanation that none of what has just been said is true.

But the reader is not often tempted to depart from his attitude of vigilance. He knows that here every word is of importance. The bywords, the quotations, the metaphors, the ready-made, pompous or pedantic expressions, the platitudes, vulgarities, mannerisms and pointless remarks with which these dialogues are cleverly studded are not, as they are in ordinary novels, distinctive signs that the author pins on the characters to make them more easily recognizable, more familiar and more "alive." They are here, one feels, what they are in reality: the resultant of numerous, entangled movements that have come up from the depths, and which anyone perceiving them from the outside takes in at a glance, but which he has neither the time nor the means to separate and name.

No doubt this method is content to make the reader constantly suspect the existence, the complexity and the variety of the inner movements. It does not make him acquainted with them, in the way that techniques which plunged him into their depths and made him navigate through their currents, could succeed in doing. But it has at least the superiority over these latter techniques of having immediately attained to perfection. And by so doing it has succeeded in giving to traditional dialogue the worst blow it has received so far.

116

Quite obviously, one day in the near future, this technique, along with all the others, will seem incapable of describing anything but appearances. And nothing could be more cheering and more stimulating than this thought. It will be the sign that all is for the best, that life goes on, and that we must not turn back, but strive to go farther forward.

Nouvelle Revue Française
January-February, 1956.

What

Birds

See

Of all the interesting subjects for meditation offered us by the attitude of the public toward literary works, and especially toward the novel, certainly one of the most interesting is the admiration, the unanimous, unreserved love of this public, which, in other respects, is so divided, so fluctuating, so capricious, for acknowledged masterpieces. This does not apply, needless to say, to readers whose admiration is based in all confidence on expert opinion, but to those to whom these works appear to be so familiar that we are forced to believe in the genuine pleasure they derive from their company.

We all know what fine qualities this pleasure is generally considered to imply in those who experience it. We ought therefore to marvel. And yet we hesitate. The admirers of these works often speak of them so strangely. . . . We are disconcerted by the unimportant details that seem to have struck them particularly, that they seem to have retained particularly: trifles that they could find quite as well in works devoid of all literary value—such as physical peculiarities, mannerisms, traits of disposition of certain characters, anecdotes, social customs, practical advice, tips on how to become successful, rules of conduct, etc. . . .—which remind us a bit of the following comment that Rilke tells of having heard while looking at a portrait of Cézanne's wife: "How could he have married such a homely woman?"; or of this one overheard in front of a Van Gogh canvas: "Poor man, you can see that he has just had his furniture attached."

But when we think it over, there is nothing very disturbing about remarks of this sort. They should rather set our minds at rest; for they are perhaps merely the familiar and somewhat off-hand manners that denote great intimacy. This emphasis on minor detail gives us perhaps to understand that these persons consider as acknowledged and only too well known what constitutes the real importance of these works. Perhaps it is out of shyness that they refrain from speaking of what is nearest their hearts; or else there is a touch of snobbishness in it, the desire—as in the case of the character in Babbitt who said he liked Rome especially for the delicious fettucine to be had in a little trattoria on the Via della Scrofa—to appear sophisticated and blasé.

In any case, there is nothing very serious in all that, nothing that would make it worth our while, by means of indiscreet intrusions, to pry into the secrecy of the eminently respectable tête-à-tête between literary masterpieces and their readers; and we should hasten to throw over this union, which is so worthy of every encouragement, the veil of modesty, confidence and respect with which we are accustomed to invest legitimate marriage if, from time to time, there did not occur something really disquieting.

Every now and then we see our most influential critics in the grip of a kind of dizziness, which is comprehensible of course in persons who are so busy reading. But then they suddenly begin to pronounce a masterpiece and praise to the skies, a work that is devoid of all literary value, as will be proven, some time later, by the indifference, then the oblivion, into which its weakness will inevitably let it slip.

In their wake, the public is carried off its feet by a veritable tidal wave which raises it to the peak of admiration and enthusiasm.

Once all bans have been lifted, it is astonishing to see with what avidity the most faithful and most enthusiastic lovers of literary masterpieces—those who, ordinarily, when faced with a new work, are so forbidding, so severe, so fastidious—devour these works as though they were the most succulent of foods; even more succulent, they confess (and why should they hide a taste that is shared by the most respected critics?), than those that are offered them by the great works of the past. Here no adaptation is necessary; we enter in without effort and immediately everything goes quite smoothly; the characters are like us, or like people we know, or else as we imagine those of our contemporaries whom we should like to know.

Their feelings, their ideas, their conflicts, the situations in which they find themselves, the problems they must solve, their hopes and their despair are all ours: we feel quite in our element in their lives. In vain a few sophisticated spirits, a few maladjusted persons express certain reservations. It is the lack of art, they say, in a way that is as vague as it is pretentious, which discommodes them. Or perhaps the weakness of style. But they are immediately snubbed; they call down upon themselves general disapproval, they arouse people's distrust and hostility. They are taxed with favoring art for art's sake. Accused of "formalism." And in reality, they only get what they deserve. For who on earth would think of laying himself open to sarcasm so clumsily as this, of treating such serious questions with such blundering frivolity?

But let several months, more often several years, go by, and we witness the following astonishing fact: not only the new readers of these novels, but their greatest admirers themselves, if they have the misfortune to commit the imprudence of rereading them, as soon as they pick up one of these books, have the same painful sensation that the birds who tried to pilfer Zeuxis' famous grapes must have had. What they see is nothing but an illusion of reality. A flat, inert copy. The characters are like wax dummies, fabricated according to the easiest, most conventional methods. Clearly, these books cannot even be used, as may certain novels of the past, as documents of their epoch, for it is hard to believe that these childish plots, these puppets that are the leading characters, and which imitate the grossest sort of semblance, could ever have had the feelings, faced the conflicts or been obliged to solve the problems that the living men of their time did.

What happened, then? And how may we explain such a metamorphosis?

It should first be observed that the authors of the works under discussion are not devoid of talent. They undoubtedly have what are usually referred to as the gifts that go to make a novelist. Not only do they know how to concoct a plot, develop action, create what is called "atmosphere," but moreover, and above all, they know how to seize and represent likeness. Every gesture their characters make, the way they smooth their hair, adjust the pleat in their trousers, light a cigarette or order a cup of coffee, as well as the things they say, the feelings they have, the ideas that cross their minds, constantly give the reader the stimulating and delightful impression of recognizing what he may have or could have observed himself. We might even say that the great good fortune of these novelists, the secret of their felicity and of that of their readers, resides in the fact that they set up their observation posts quite naturally at the exact spot on which the reader too is located. Neither on this side, where the authors and readers of cheap serials are to be found, nor on the far side, in that secret twilight zone, that confused seething, in which our actions and our words are forming. No, at the very place where we ourselves are accustomed to be, when we want to give a rather clear account, to ourselves or to others, of our feelings or our impressions. And indeed, if we are to judge by the conversations of persons having wide experience of psychological matters, as soon as these novelists begin to be confidential or catty, to describe themselves or their neighbors, they are more apt to be on the far side, only a little more in depth.

Thanks to this favorable position, they in-

spire confidence in their readers, who have the
impression of being quite at home, among objects that are quite familiar. A feeling of
friendliness, solidarity and also of gratitude
unites them with this novelist, who is so like
them, who understands so well what they themselves feel, but who, at the same time, being a
little more discerning than they are, more atten-
tive, more experienced, shows them a little more
about themselves and about others than they
believe they know, and leads them, just excited
enough by a very slight effort, but never tired or
discouraged by too great an effort, never slowed
down or impeded in their pace, toward what
they hope to obtain when they start to read a
novel: help in their loneliness, a description of
their own situations, disclosures about the
secret sides of other people's lives, advice filled
with wisdom, correct solutions to the conflicts
from which they are suffering, broadening of
their experience, an impression of living other
lives.

These needs seem so natural, and the con-
tentment derived from satisfying them is so
great, that we can understand the impatience
provoked in these readers by the spoil-sports

128

who, just when they are feeling most gratified, come and talk to them about "art" or "style." What difference does it make to them if these works are not destined to last? And if, one day when, with the help of these books, their difficulties will have been overcome, their situations altered, their sentiments changed and their curiosity aroused by other ways of living, interest in these books should wane and the excitement they stirred up die down, there is nothing to be said against this, and to regret it would be a mistake. Why stock works with an eye to an unknown future, however imperishable they may appear to be, when what is most urgent is to give immediate, effective aid to the humanity of one's time. For a book to wear out when it has served its purpose is only natural and sound. We throw it away and replace it by another.

And this opinion would be so obviously the part of wisdom that no one would dream of disputing it, if it were not for one very disquieting point, which is, the painful impression, as soon as the excitement these works have stirred up dies down, that what they described was not reality. Or rather, that it was only a surface reality, nothing but the flattest, most commonplace sort of semblance. More commonplace even, and more cursory, contrary to what it had seemed at first, than what we ourselves perceive, however hurried and absent-minded we may be.

Everyone knows to what extent, in our haste, we can be ignorant and credulous, obliged as we are continually to do what presses most, to be guided by the grossest of appearances. It suffices to recall what a revelation the interior monologue was for us; the wariness with which we regarded and at times still regard the efforts of Henry James or Proust to take apart the delicate wheelworks of our inner mechanisms; with what readiness we consent to believe that a certain cipher code—such as psychoanalysis—when applied to the immense mobile mass we call our "heart of hearts," in which almost anything may be found, can cover it entirely and give an account of all its movements; and with what satisfaction, what a feeling of deliverance, we let ourselves be convinced, and have most of us remained convinced, that this "heart of hearts" which, quite recently, still offered such a fertile field for discovery, did not exist, was nothing: empty space, so much air.

But what makes us lose all sense of judgment, and vastly increases our credulity, is a certain need that impels us to look to novels for the previously mentioned satisfactions, and which we shall have to qualify as extra-literary, since they can be furnished us quite as well by works that are devoid of literary value as by those that have attained to the peak of perfection.

Here our already great suggestibility and malleability become really astonishing: in our impatience to experience the pleasures that these books so generously offer us, we try to recognize ourselves in the crudest of images, we make ourselves as inconsistent as possible so as to flow easily into the already prepared molds that are held out to us; in our own eyes, we become so bloodless and so empty that, however cramped these casts may be, it seems to us that they hold us entirely. Indeed, there is not so much as a fortune-teller's printed slip from which we do not derive an impression of miraculous self-recognition, from the moment it raises in us a vague hope of finding consolation and foretelling the future.

Any novel, consequently, that succeeds in satisfying this dangerous passion becomes for us, at little cost, the very image of life, a work of the most powerful realism, which we compare with the best of the classics, with the most highly accomplished writings.

Just here our worst suspicions are confirmed. For confusion such as this to be possible, these then must be the satisfactions that admirers of first-class works demand of them. We may legitimately believe, for instance, that most of Proust's readers liked him, and still like him, for reasons that have little to do with what constitutes his real worth, and that are not very different from those for which their parents or their grandparents liked Georges Ohnet.

It is even, we must now conclude, precisely that which has grown most outmoded in good books, which has been most imitated, and is consequently most commonly accepted and taken for granted, that brings them closer in the eyes of their admirers to spurious good novels. Like the latter, they no longer present any obstacles, they require almost no more effort, and they permit the reader, comfortably settled in his own familiar world, to glide weakly along toward dangerous delights.

And yet good books are the salvation of the reader, in spite of himself. For they present a difference from the others that it would be a mistake to regard as negligible: they bear re-reading.

But it should not be thought that what separates the authors of these two kinds of works is above all a difference of talent. If we look closely, it is rather a radical difference of attitude toward the object upon which all their efforts must be concentrated and, consequently, a total difference of method. This is so true that we ought to put even contemporary writers in the same category with these earlier writers who are still read, if their attitude and working methods are the same, and whatever their talent —talent being about equally divided between the two categories—or however uncertain the future of their books.

If we had to designate all of these writers by one name, it would have to be that of "realist," in opposition to the others to whom, however paradoxical and outrageous this may seem to them, the name "formalist" is exactly applicable.

But, people will ask, what do you mean by a realistic writer? Well, quite simply—and it could not be otherwise—a writer who, above all —however great his desire to amuse his contemporaries, to reform them, to instruct them or to fight for their emancipation—applies himself, while making an effort to cheat as little as possible and neither to trim nor smooth anything for the purpose of overcoming contradictions and complexities, to seizing with all the sincerity of which he is capable, to scrutinizing as far as his sharpness of vision will permit him to see, what appears to him to be reality.

To achieve this, he works unceasingly to rid what he sees of all the matrix of preconceived ideas and ready-made images that encase it, as also of all the surface reality that everyone can easily see and which, for want of anything better, everyone uses; and occasionally he succeeds in attaining to something that is thus far unknown, which it seems to him he is the first to have seen. When he tries to bring to light this fragment of reality that is his own, he frequently notices that the methods of his predecessors, which were created by them for their own ends, can no longer serve his purpose. He therefore rejects them without hesitation and applies himself to finding new ones for his own usage. Little does he care if, at first, they disconcert or irritate his readers.

His passion for this reality is so great and so sincere that he shrinks from no sacrifice it may entail. Indeed, he accepts the greatest of all those that a writer may be led to make: loneliness and the moments of doubt and distress that attend it (and which have caused some of the greatest to make such statements as: "People will understand me in 1880,"[1] or, "I'll win my suit in the Court of Appeals,"[2] which it is unfair to interpret as vague childish dreams of posthumous conquest and glory, for they show these writers' need to keep up their courage, to maintain their confidence, to persuade themselves that what they were practically alone in seeing was true, and not a mirage or, as Cézanne came to believe, the result of defective vision).

Style (whose harmony and visible beauty are such a constant, dangerous temptation for writers) is for this writer merely an instrument, the only value of which is that of serving to extract and embrace as closely as possible the fragment of reality that he is trying to lay bare. All desire to write "beautifully" for the pleasure of doing so, to give aesthetic enjoyment to him-

[1] Stendhal.
[2] Baudelaire.

self or to his readers, is quite inconceivable for him; style, from his standpoint, being capable of beauty only in the sense that an athlete's gesture is beautiful; the better it is adapted to its purpose, the greater the beauty. And this beauty, which is composed of vigor, precision, vivacity, suppleness, boldness and economy of means, is merely the expression of its effectiveness.

This reality, to which all of these writers held fast with such undivided, sincere passion, once a certain number of them had succeeded in seizing it, whether in its metaphysical, poetic, psychological or social aspects—at times it was their good fortune, or rather their compensation, to seize it in all these aspects at one time—nothing was ever able to destroy or even debase it. Though the ideas are often out of date, the sentiments only too well known or outmoded, the characters cruder than those we have since come to know; though there is nothing unpredictable in either the development or the outcome of the plot; beneath the heavy apparatus that these novelists were obliged to construct to capture this reality, and in which today it seems to us to be imprisoned, we sense it like

136

a hard core that lends its cohesion and firmness to the entire novel, like a source of heat that radiates throughout its parts something that everyone recognizes but that no one is able to designate otherwise than by such vague terms as "truth" or "life." This is the reality to which we always return, in spite of our momentary betrayals and deviations, thus proving that, when all is said and done, we too prize it above all else.

This is not at all the case with the formalists and their writings. And they are the ones to whom this term of formalists is most applicable, even though they generally use it only in derision to designate the writers in the opposite camp, reserving for themselves, however strange such blindness may seem, the name of "realists."

It is quite obvious, however, that reality is not their main interest, but form, always, form invented by others, and from which a magnetic force makes them unable ever to break away. At times this is the harmonious, pure form in which so-called "classic" writers tightly enclosed objects created from one single piece of the dense, heavy matter upon which their efforts were concentrated. The fact that these objects, having been disintegrated into countless particles, are now nothing but an immense fluctuating mass which it is no longer possible to enclose between these spare outlines matters little to these formalists. What they strive to achieve above all else is the elegant simplicity of the classic form, even though the form that they contrive to create is today nothing but a thin, empty shell that will crack under the slightest pressure.

At other times, abandoning harmony and quiet distinction, they adopt a form whose essential characteristic is that it tries to obtain "likeness." This it succeeds in doing with no difficulty, being so constituted that today it is hardly able to seize upon anything whatsoever that is still little known, or unusual, and consequently, to start with, improbable or disconcerting. This was not the case formerly, at the time when it was invented for the purpose of disclosing what was still unknown and hidden. But since then, the unknown and hidden having taken up their abode beyond its reach, it has been emptied of its living content, and today only serves to conceal rather gross, schematic appearances: characters reduced to over-simplified types, conventional sentiments, actions based less on sincere experience than on the fictional convention this form prescribes, dialogues that recall less those we might hear if we listened very attentively and without bias to what we ourselves say and what is said about us, than those that usually take place between the characters in novels of this kind.

Nothing but habit of long standing, that has become second nature, in addition to our submission to all generally accepted conventions, our continual absent-mindedness and haste, and, above all, the avidity that impels us to devour the appetizing foods these novels offer, make us agree to let ourselves be taken in by the deceptive surfaces that this form sets shimmering before our eyes.

When we see the hold that the formalists have succeeded in getting on the novel today, we cannot help agreeing with those who declare that it is the most underprivileged of all the arts.

Of course it is hard to imagine novelists permitting themselves to undertake anything that would be comparable to the evasion attempted by painters when, with one blast, they blew up the entire classic system of conventions—which had come to serve less to reveal, as it once did, than to conceal what, to their eyes, was the real object of painting—abolishing subject and perspective, and wresting the spectator from the familiar appearances in which he had been accustomed to find satisfactions that had ceased to have much in common with painting. True, this evasion was short-lived. The new formalists, imitators of these painters, were not long in changing these living forms into dead ones, and the spectators soon replaced the facile pleasures they had derived from the true-to-nature subjects of earlier painting by those to be had from looking at agreeable, decorative patterns.

But how could a novelist free himself from the necessity of having a subject, characters and a plot? For no matter how hard he tried to isolate the fragment of reality that he was striving to grasp, he could not keep it from integrating with some character whose familiar figure presented in simple, precise lines, the practiced eye of the reader would immediately reconstitute and rig out with a "personality," in which he would recognize one of the types he so relishes and which, by virtue of its very true-to-nature, "live" aspect, would absorb most of his attention. In fact, however the author may try to maintain this character in a motionless state, in order to concentrate his own and the reader's attention on the barely perceptible tremors in which it seems to him that the reality he would like to disclose has taken refuge, he will not succeed in keeping it from moving just enough for the reader to see in its movements a plot whose ins and outs he will follow with curiosity, while impatiently awaiting the ending.

And so, no matter what the novelist may do, he cannot distract the reader's attention from all sorts of objects that just any novel, whether good or bad, can furnish him.

Many critics, in fact, encourage this absent-mindedness and frivolity in readers by giving in to it themselves, thus fostering confusion.

Indeed, it is astonishing to see with what complacency they dwell upon anecdotal features, relate the "story" and discuss the "characters," appraising their verisimilitude and examining their morality. But it is with regard to style that their attitude is strangest. If a novel is written in a style that recalls the classics, they usually attribute the qualities of *Adolph* or *The Princess of Cleve* to the subject matter, however indigent, that this style covers. If, on the contrary, one of these novels with such lifelike characters and thrilling plots should happen to be written in a flat, slipshod style, they mention this fault indulgently, as an imperfection that is to be regretted, no doubt, but that is of little importance; only the fastidious will be shocked by it and it in no way affects the real value of the book: something, in other words, as superficial and insignificant as a small wart or an ordinary pimple on a handsome, noble face. In reality, however, it is more like the telltale pimple that appears on the body of a plague victim, the plague in this case being nothing else but an attitude that is hardly sincere and hardly honest toward reality.

But the confusion reaches its peak when, as a result of the novel's tendency to be an art that always lags behind the others, and that is less capable of breaking away from outmoded forms that have been emptied of all living content, people want to make it into a weapon of combat that will serve the revolution or maintain and perfect revolutionary gains.

This leads to strange results that constitute a rather disquieting threat not only to the novel

—which, after all, would not be very serious, and to which, if need be, we might become resigned—but to the revolution to be achieved, to the masses it is intended to liberate, and to the safeguard of gains made by a revolution that has already taken place. Indeed, the satisfactions we termed extra-literary, advice, examples, moral and social education, etc. . . . which it is in the very nature of the novel to mete out generously to its readers, having become the essential raison d'être of the novel, we witness a reversal of all values: to forge a revolutionary weapon from the novel, it is necessary to use the very things that make it subservient to an academic, set form: characters that are like wax dolls, as lifelike as possible, so "alive," in fact, that at first glance the reader probably feels like poking them to see if they will blink, the way we should like to do to the figures in waxworks museums—all this being needed to make the readers feel at ease, to allow them to identify themselves without difficulty with the characters and, in this way, to relive their own "situations," their own sufferings, their own conflicts.

But "types" that are even more crudely constructed, the simplest of outlines, a positive, irreproachable hero and a traitor, will do even better since, for the masses, whose sensitivity and clear-sightedness these novelists greatly underestimate, they are either magnificent bird snares or very effective scarecrows. A plot that moves forward briskly according to the rules of the old-fashioned novel will make these puppets pirouette about and create the kind of facile excitement that succeeds so well in sustaining the reader's flagging attention. And since the style, which is a sort of digest style, the same in all of these books, never serves to reveal a new reality, never makes a crack in the varnish of conventional appearances that covers it, but flows sluggishly along without encountering the slightest obstacle, coating smooth surfaces—well, there is no doubt that this style will never be too commonplace, too simple or too fluent, since these are qualities that can make a work accessible to the great masses of people and help them to swallow down these substantial foods that it is one's duty to offer them.

Thus, in the name of moral imperatives, we end by accepting the immorality that, in literature, results from a negligent, conformist, hardly sincere, hardly honest attitude toward reality.

By presenting readers with a reality that is mutilated and a snare, an indigent, flat appearance in which, once the first moments of excitement and hope have passed, they find nothing that really constitutes their lives, neither the real difficulties with which they must cope nor the real conflicts they have to face, we alienate them and arouse their distrust, we discourage them in their efforts to find in literature the essential satisfaction that it alone can give them: a deeper, more complex, clearer, truer knowledge of what they are, of their circumstances and their lives, than they can acquire alone.

Here and there, by drawing upon a sincere, living experience whose roots go deep into the unconscious source from which all creative effort springs, completely shattering the old, sclerosed forms, writers have discovered and are still discovering the aspect of reality that can render direct and effective service to the propagation and victory of revolutionary ideas. But it can also happen (even in a society that applies itself to being the fairest and best designed for assuring the harmonious development of all its members: this may be stated as a certainty without any risk of being mistaken) that isolated, maladjusted, lonely individuals, morbidly attached to their childhood, withdrawn into themselves and cultivating a more or less conscious taste for a certain form of defeat, by giving in to an apparently useless obsession, succeed in digging up and laying bare a fragment of reality that is still unknown.

Their works, which seek to break away from all that is prescribed, conventional and dead, to turn toward what is free, sincere and alive, will necessarily, sooner or later, become ferments of emancipation and progress.

We can understand that it should have seemed and should still seem inopportune to allow the masses, who had been maintained in ignorance for centuries, to have too rapid access to a deeper knowledge of the complexities and contradictions of their lives: this would tend to divert them from the task of construction on which their existence depends, and which requires their concentrated attention as well as their entire effort.

However, the indifference, the increasing detachment not only of their leaders but of the masses themselves with regard to literary works that lack vitality, that are fabricated according

146

to the old-fashioned methods of sclerosed formalism, and the interest shown by these same masses in the great works of the past that are being revealed to them, prove that the time is not far off when these maladjusted, lonely individuals should not only be allowed to work without being discouraged, but should even be encouraged to give in to their obsessions.

January, 1956.